Solstice Publishing Presents

The Food of Love

2015

Cover Art:
Michelle Crocker

http://mlcdesigns4you.weebly.com/

Publisher's Note:

This is a work of fiction. All names, characters, places, and events are the work of the author's imagination.

Any resemblance to real persons, places, or events is coincidental.

Solstice Publishing - www.solsticepublishing.com

The Way to a Man's Heart
Mya O'Malley

Chapter One

"Are you sure you have to go away on Valentine's Day, of all days?" Sophia twirled her soft auburn hair through her fingers. "Why can't you just tell Hank that you have other plans?'

"First of all, it's Tom; Hank hasn't been around in ages. Secondly, I really like him, so no; I'm going away that weekend." Susan exhaled deeply.

Protruding her lower lip, Sophia batted her eyes and gazed at her sister. The little trick had earned her tons of attention as a child and usually resulted in Sophia getting her own way. Her "big sister" was six minutes older and took the role of older sister seriously, too seriously. Identical twins from the top of their auburn heads to the bottom of their size eight feet.

"Nope. Not this time. I'm sorry to leave you alone on Valentine's Day, but it's just another weekend; look at it that way."

"Well... if it's just another weekend, then why don't you tell Hank... excuse me, Tom, that you'll reschedule." Waiting for the inevitable response to follow, Sophia held her breath.

"You need to get out there again, try something new. Don't let your experience with Jerry ruin you for all men. You've got plenty of time to find a date for Valentine's Day if that's what you really want," Susan explained as she gathered up her scarf and coat.

She did have plenty of time, didn't she? That gave Sophia pause as she mentally calculated how much time she had before Valentine's Day.

As if reading her mind, which the twins had a knack for doing, Susan responded. "A little over a month."

"What is that men want anyway? I mean, they're very complicated creatures. I've tried meeting a nice man but they all turn out to be jerks," Sophia exclaimed, rising to her feet to follow Susan to the door.

"You overcomplicate everything, little sis. When the time is right, you'll know it. Now, excuse me or I'll be late for work."

"Right." Sophia saluted her sister as she rushed out the door. Sophia padded down the hallway to the bathroom to get ready for her own job. Maybe Susan was right, perhaps she should rent a movie and get some popcorn for Valentine's Day, spend the night by herself, she would have the entire apartment to herself with Susan being gone for the weekend. Taylor crept out of her bedroom, meowing to announce his presence. The ragdoll cat seemed to be her only company lately.

Cringing inwardly, Sophia shook her head firmly. "No way. There's no way that I'm going to become a cat lady alone on Valentine's Day. Picking up her pace a bit, Sophia felt a spring in her step. Known for being stubborn and determined, this girl wasn't going to give up. Come hell or high water, Sophia would have that date on Valentine's Day.

***

Throughout her workday, Sophia racked her brain, thinking of inventive ways that she could meet that man. The bar scene? Nah, she had been there, done that. The last thing that she wanted or needed was to hook up with a man who took up drinking as a hobby. Everyone always claimed that, hey, you could meet the man if your dreams in the grocery store. Imagine that, *excuse me, is that romaine lettuce or red leaf that you have there?'*

Chucking to herself, Beth, her friend and partner at the day care center touched her shoulder. "Sophia, Terrance

4

needs to use the bathroom and I have to grab the snacks in back."

"What? Oh, sorry. I guess I kind of got lost in my thoughts there for a second." Shaking off her brain fog, she sought out Terrance and walked him to the bathroom.

"Now, you're fine. I'll be right here, I promise." The blond haired toddler gazed up at Sophia with huge blue eyes. Terrance had been experiencing separation anxiety the last several weeks and needed constant assurance that somebody would be with him at all times, that included walking him to the bathroom and speaking to him the entire time he was behind closed doors.

"I'm still here. Miss Beth is getting your snack; I wonder what you're having today. Mmm, I'm sure it'll be delicious." Emphasizing the word delicious, Sophia heard the little voice responding from the other side of the door.

"You're a natural." Beth 's voice came from behind her, hustling past with her arms full.

"Yeah, right." Sophia actually snorted. That would be something, having a child now. Truth be told, she was twenty-seven years old, certainly old enough to have a family. It couldn't be that her biological clock was ticking already. Plenty if time for children, she had been telling herself lately.

The sound of the toilet flushing jarred Sophia out of her thoughts once more. Terrance opened the door and rewarded Sophia with the warmest smile she had ever seen. "Thank you, Miss Sophia." And, yes, her heart melted.

"Let's go, little man." Grabbing for his hand, Sophia led Terrance to the table where his snack of yogurt and a banana was waiting for him.

After making the rounds of opening impossible juice boxes and tearing open bags of miscellaneous food items, Sophia and Beth finally had a chance to sit. Beth fidgeted in her seat, eyes darting around the room.

"Are you okay? You seem tired. No offense or

anything, but you looked exhausted all week." Sophia glanced at her friend, who suddenly looked several shades of green. Without a word, Beth darted toward the bathroom. Sophia's jaw opened, wondering if her friend had that stomach virus that had been going around. *But wait, wasn't that last month?* A creeping thought penetrated Sophia's head. No, it couldn't be, but it made sense. Beth had refused her favorite beer last week when they went out to dinner and she was making numerous trips to the bathroom. With wide eyes, Sophia put all of the facts together. A grim looking Beth headed back into the main room.

"You're going to have a baby, aren't you." It was more of a statement than a question.

"You hit the nail on the head." Beth turned to her co-worker and fell into her open arms.

"Wow. I mean, wow. I just can't believe it, you, being a mom."

"Is it all that hard to believe?" Beth questioned, her head cocked to the side.

"Not at all, you'll make a wonderful mother." Sophia meant every word; her friend would be the perfect doting mother. "Any baby will be lucky to have you for a mother; congratulations."

"Thank you, I appreciate it. Now, if only I felt better." Beth's complexion appeared slightly better.

"Hang in there, kid. I'm sure you'll feel better soon." Placing an arm around her friend, Sophia thought about that ticking biological clock of her own.

Chapter Two

Staying at home by himself was simply not an option for Trent tonight. The past few Saturdays he had rented a movie, fiddled around in the garage, and perused dating sites on his laptop. His buddy, Billy, swore by the popular online dating site Heart to Heart, but Trent was having no part of it. Posting his photo for all the world to see seemed an act of desperation and this boy was not desperate. Unlucky in love lately, yes, but not desperate. Grabbing his jacket, he headed out the door to Jay's Pub. Jason O'Rourke was one of his oldest friends, from grade school in fact. He owned the pub with his wife who was forever coming up with charming ideas to draw customers in. Tonight was Saturday night so that would be karaoke night, amusing to watch, but terrifying to participate in. Never in a million years would he hang out in a bar alone on a Saturday night, but visiting one of his best friends was certainly not out of the question.

Taking a trip down memory lane did nothing to improve his mood. Sure, Cynthia had dumped him after two years of marriage and, yes, it was true that he was better off without a cheating bride, and it was also true that it was a good thing he'd never had children with Cynthia, but the ache was still ever-present in his heart. Nobody liked getting dumped, period. For a while, the fact had caused some real damage to his self-esteem. A lying, cheating wife could do that to you. After his experience, Trent knew that it was essential that any woman he dated withstood his criteria. Number One: The woman could not be a cheater, ever, even in her past. Number Two: His date could not be caught in a lie. Lies led to deception and deception led to… well, bad places. Knowing full well that no woman in her right mind would admit to either one of the offenses, Trent swore that he would guard his heart, keep one eye open, so to speak, until he felt safe enough to give his heart away, if that was even possible again. Trent was relieved on one hand that he didn't have a life-long bind with Cynthia, but on the other hand, he had always wanted children, and plenty of them. Three children would be perfect, he mused, but he was thirty–two years old and he kind of pictured that little boy or girl in his life at this point.

Jay's was packed as usual on a weekend night. Stealing a glance around, Trent noticed exactly one bar stool open at the end of the bar, right near the stage. At least he would get a good view of the karaoke tonight.

"Hey, man. Glad you made it. What'll it be tonight? The usual?" Jason plopped an ice-cold draft of beer right in front of him.

"Um, sure. Is the kitchen still open?" Glancing at the time on his cell, he knew that it would be a close call.

"Pizza, wings, anything I can throw on the grill would be fine." Jason shrugged his shoulders.

The one thing, the *only* thing that Trent missed about Cynthia was her cooking. Boy, she could cook. From entrées to desserts and everything in between, she was a master in the kitchen. Developing the third criteria in his head, Trent decided right then and there that the woman he ended up with would need to be a good cook.

"Hey, there are some really cute girls here for karaoke tonight; check out the blonde near the door." Jason winked at his long time friend. Spinning his head around, Trent took in the lanky blonde and her friends. Laughter could be heard from the group and it appeared that they were all having a grand time. Blond hair? Realizing that his criteria was becoming more complicated by the minute, Trent added a new rule, the woman cannot be a blonde. Realizing that he was acting childish, he didn't care. Cynthia had blond hair. This time around, maybe he'd go for a brunette or even a redhead.

"Nah. Too young," Trent announced turning back to

face his friend and checking the hockey score on the flat screen television.

"You're hopeless, man." Jason wiped the bar in front of him with a damp cloth.

Swigging on his glass of beer, Trent chuckled softly. "So I've been told."

***

Taylor swirled his tail around Sophia's legs. Gazing up at her adoringly, the feline meowed loudly. "Yeah, yeah. I know what you want. Even you have an ulterior motive." Rising from the couch, Sophia grabbed the remote control and paused the sappy but irresistible chick-flick she was completely engrossed in. Padding into the kitchen, she opened the cabinet and grasped the cat treats. "There, are you happy that you disturbed me now?" A thankful mew escaped from the cat's mouth as it crunched greedily on the treat. A local magazine on the kitchen table caught Sophia's eye. The monthly issue displayed Valentine's Day candy and flowers on the front cover. Drawing closer, Sophia clucked her tongue in disgust. But she couldn't help herself, she was compelled to open the magazine.

"Hmph." Sophia expelled. "*Book your reservations early, the most romantic night of your life...* blah, blah, blah. Reading the headlines of advertisements brought on that twitch of loneliness again. Shaking her head from side to side, Sophia spoke aloud. "Overrated. This holiday is totally overrated." She was about to close the magazine when a bright red ad caught her eye. *Don't have a Valentine yet? Don't despair... Singles Cooking Class. Who knows? You might just find love or at the very least, learn how to cook with that loving touch.* And so it went, the ad held Sophia's attention and as much as she didn't want to admit it, it intrigued her. Cooking? That was one area where she Susan did not have anything in common. Susan was an excellent cook; it was like she baked with magic. Just thinking about her Christmas press sugar cookies was enough to make Sophia drool right there on the spot. Any talent in the kitchen did not find its way to Sophia. Somehow their genes must have crossed signals in that area. Placing the article down softly on the table, Sophia walked away. "Nah." Within seconds, she was back at the table finding the page again. "Page 103, here it is." The cooking class was offered at a neighboring restaurant it appeared. She had heard of the restaurant but had never been there as it was about twenty minutes away. Twenty minutes wasn't too long of a drive, though. Reading further, she took in the details of the class. Weekly one-hour sessions leading up to Valentine's Day. The final class or "final exam" as they called it, was a two-hour event, wrapping up on the Thursday night right before Valentine's Day. It appeared the "final exam" would involve teaching the rest of the class a mastered dish or dessert of your choice for all to enjoy, as kind of a party for the last day. Something about the ad pulled at her. Sophia could almost hear her twin sister urging her to attend. *Go for it, open up your possibilities.* It was that uncanny sense of telepathy that many twins shared.

"Oh, what the heck!" Dialing the number of the restaurant, Sophia mentally prepared her list of questions.

"Jay's Pub. Can I help you?" A man's deep voice boomed from the receiver. Sounds of laughter and loud music could be heard in the background.

A pub? That's odd. Sophia continued. "Yes, I was looking for information on your cooking class?" She posed it as a question, because perhaps she had the wrong number, what kind of a pub holds cooking classes?

"Yeah, that would be my wife's department. Hold on a sec." The man called to his wife as Sophia scribbled on her notepad, prepared to take down the information.

Seconds went by and a woman's voice came through. "Yes, you're interested in the cooking class?"

Sophia gathered the information about the singles

cooking class. This was the first time that the class was offered but the woman claimed that several men had signed up for the class and that she was expecting more. Hesitating a brief second, the woman assured her that, yes, this was a chance to meet men, and, yes, this class was suitable for beginners. "Sign me up, it's not like I have any other plans for the next several Thursdays."

"That's the spirit." The owner of Jay's applauded while she happily took down Sophia's information. "So the class starts this Thursday at six o'clock, your material fees are included with the tuition for class and you're all set."

"How does that work, at the pub, I mean?" Curiosity got the best of Sophia as she pictured a cooking class centered around a crowded bar.

"We use the kitchen here, it's rather large and I figured that you guys could always join up in the bar area after class and enjoy a drink if you'd like." It did sound like a unique idea.

"Well, great, I'll see you on Thursday. What was your name again?"

"Oops, sorry. I'm not usually this rude, I'm Jackie, my husband, Jason, and I own Jay's. I'll be there on Thursday, I'm the instructor."

"Great. I look forward to meeting you." Sophia had a good feeling about this, if nothing else it would be an experience.

With a grin, she settled back down on the couch and hit the play button.

Chapter Three

"You're doing *what?*" Susan called from her bedroom. "Are you sure that it's a beginning class?" Susan appeared freshly showered with a towel wrapped around her head.

"Very funny." Sophia retorted.

"I'm not trying to be funny, I'm serious. No offense, but you can't even boil water."

"Thanks for being so encouraging. You know, I even heard your voice urging me to try this, to try something new and exciting." Slamming a coffee mug down on the table, Sophia felt red reach her cheeks.

"Okay, I'm sorry. I just want you to be prepared, is all. I actually think it's a good thing." Sidling up to her sister, Susan reached out to rub her shoulder.

Backing away, Sophia turned her eyes away.

"Ouch." Susan exclaimed. "I said I was sorry."

"Fine. I don't want to hear any more about it though. I'm taking the class to try to meet a guy and, who knows? Maybe I'll learn a thing or two about cooking while I'm at it." Sophia announced, her head held high.

"Atta girl, go for it. Although perhaps if you go into this with the intention of learning to cook first and taking the chance that you may meet a man, you might learn more from your experience."

"What fun would that be?" Sophia had no desire to learn how to cook; her motivating factor was to meet a man. Susan shook her head and wandered back to her bedroom.

***

He had to be crazy, the way that he let Jackie and Jason talk him into signing up for that Valentine's Day singles cooking class, he could barely boil water for God's sake. Jackie had promised him that plenty of single women would be taking the class. Wasn't one of the criteria on his list for dating that the woman should know how to cook? Chances were strong that a woman taking a beginner's cooking class wouldn't be that skilled when it came to cooking. Jackie had brushed that thought aside with a swipe of her hand telling him that many of the women did indeed have experience but were looking to meet a man. So he had signed up for the ridiculous class and Jackie wouldn't even let him pay for it. *It's on us,* she had shared with a wink.

It was Thursday evening and he still couldn't believe that he was actually taking a cooking class of all things. What does one wear to a singles cooking class? Shifting his dress shirts to the side, he searched his closet for something masculine, but not too much so. *Hmm, this should do.* It was a gray flannel that was just new enough to look presentable, but not in a flashy kind of way.

Sighing loudly, Trent took a last look in the mirror headed for the door. *Who knows?* Trent thought to himself, *If this doesn't work out, at least I might learn a thing or two about cooking.* Laughing aloud, Trent knew he was fooling himself, His interest in learning how to cook ranked right up there with his interest in the ballet. Humming along to an old tune on the radio, he felt a twinge of nervousness as he drew closer to Jay's. This was why he hadn't dated much since the divorce, he hated the first meetings, getting to know someone, that awkwardness. Pulling into the parking lot he almost turned around and went back home. Jason and Jackie would never let him live that one down, though.

Approaching the door to the pub, Trent took a deep breath and put his best foot forward. The sound of music from the jukebox filled the air but otherwise it was pretty quiet. What else would you expect for a Thursday evening at six o'clock?

"Hey!" Jackie scrambled to her feet and wrapped Trent in a fierce hug. "I am so glad that you made it. Look, there's already several attractive women in there."

"Hmm. Anyone that would seem my type?" Trent ventured. The grim line formed on Jackie's lips said it all "Great."

"But they're not all here yet; I'm expecting one more woman and another man yet." Jackie explained, a hopeful look set in her eyes.

"Fine, fine." Trent peeled his heavy jacket off and placed it on a barstool. Before he had a chance to sit, Jackie informed him that he should head straight for the kitchen. Grabbing his jacket off the stool, Jackie took it from him and ushered him into the kitchen.

Approximately five women and three other men sat around a large table in the back of the kitchen. Taking a seat in between a man and an older woman, he resigned himself to the fact that this was probably a huge waste of time. Scanning the women in the group, he was disappointed to find that although they were all attractive in their own way, not one of them was his type at all. There was the woman who appeared to be at least ten years older than him, an overly made up blonde and the list went on. Trent didn't consider himself to be a shallow man at all, quite the contrary, but he also knew instantly that these women were not going to incite any interest in him. A straggler appeared in the doorway within a few minutes, an older man who just might be a good fit for the older woman. Well, at least somebody might meet that special someone here.

Ten minutes went by as Trent focused his gaze on the wooden clock hanging on the wall beside him. Jackie was in all of her glory with her bright red apron on and a gigantic smile lighting up her face. There had to be some way out of this, he mentally calculated different ways to inform Jackie that this class wasn't for him.

"I am so sorry!" The sound of her voice jolted Trent out of his bothersome thoughts. *Wow*. She burst through the door, cheeks flushed and dark auburn hair mussed up, strands covering her eyes. His heart rate sped up just a bit.

"You must be Sophia." Jackie's grin reached her eyes as she took the woman's coat from her. She was lean with slight curves in all the right places. Trent gulped as the woman took a seat two spots over from him. What was wrong with him? He couldn't even sneak a glance at this woman for fear of giving his innermost thoughts away.

"Part of the class involves working with a partner. The partner you will be assigned to, yes, assigned to, will be your partner for the entirety of the classes from here on in." Perhaps Jackie should have been a teacher; she had a natural knack for speaking in front of the class and enunciating her directions in a clear, firm way. Groans could be heard from around the table as Trent wondered himself why grown adults weren't permitted to choose their own partner for the class. Jackie did fancy herself a matchmaker, though, Trent recalled with a chuckle.

"Now, now." Jackie's voice projected not unlike his tenth grade teacher, Mrs. Park. "The reason for this is simple, I don't want any person in this room to feel as if he or she is that last little boy or girl not picked in gym class. Nobody likes that feeling and I won't permit it in my class." More groans all around. A soft, feminine chuckle came from a seat nearby. Stealing a glance at the woman, Sophia, he noticed that her face lit up.

"I happen to think that's perfect." Sophia's eyes locked with Trent's as he swore the woman blushed right down to her toes.

"Thanks, Sophia," Jackie exclaimed, making her way around the table to pair people off. Trying his best to send a subliminal message to Jackie, his heart practically did cartwheels when his partner was announced. "Trent, you'll be with Sophia here."

The two locked eyes again and smiled coyly at each other. Trent took the liberty of moving closer to Sophia and the men and women paired up. One person, the overly made up blonde, stood alone.

"Terry, you'll be my partner." Jackie scooted the woman to the front of the table. "Don't look so disappointed, Terry, we have another young man joining us next week and he just might be your type." Winking at Terry, the other woman lifted her face with a smile.

"Hi, Sophia," Trent's voice came out as a squeak. "It's nice to meet you." A pair of sparkling hazel eyes bore into him. Why was it suddenly so hot in here? Getting through this class in one piece might prove to be more of a challenge than he had bargained for. The last time a woman looked at him like that had ended up in a failed marriage. *Something tells me I'm out of my mind, sitting next to this woman.*

***

"So as we all know, the way to a man's heart is thorough is stomach." Jackie joked lovingly while Sophia cringed. If that were true, she was in real trouble. After class ended, the adults dispersed, some heading for the bar while others made their way home. All in all, the night was shaping up to be much more exciting than Sophia had counted on. An awkward silence filled the air as she grabbed her jacket and said goodbye to her partner, Trent.

"Oh. I mean… you're not staying for a drink?" The way that man fumbled over his words was adorable, he had been doing it all evening.

Gazing up at a pair of sexy brown eyes, Sophia felt a tingle course through her body. She had been hoping that he would ask her to stay for a drink. "Um, sure. Are you?"

His wavy dark hair fell in his eyes as he guided her toward the bar area. "Sure, why not." *Why not is right,* Sophia thought to herself, hiding a quick smile by biting her lip.

Trent ordered drinks for the two of them and that undeniable spark of electricity filled the air around them.

An old blues song filled the air with emotion so thick Sophia could almost taste it. Minutes melted into hours as the couple spoke about anything and everything. Sophia couldn't recall when last she'd had such a great time. Her sister's image filled her head, giving her a silent thumbs-up.

"I hate to break this up, but we're closing soon." Jason chuckled as he gestured around the otherwise empty bar. Sophia was surprised to see that she and Trent were the only customers left.

"Wow. I'm sorry, man. I'll settle up the bill and get out of your way." Trent dug through his pockets and paid the bill, rejecting the money which had Sophia offered for her share of the bill.

"Can I walk you to your car?" Trent offered his hand to her and Sophia swore that her heart was doing little flips inside of her chest. Darkness enveloped them as they made their way to Sophia's car. She fumbled with the keys, preparing to open her door.

"Hey, Sophia?" Trent's voice was husky as he took hold of her elbow.

Words weren't necessary as Sophia gazed up, locking her gaze into his deep brown eyes. Her body tingled as Trent leaned down from his full height of around six feet and placed the softest kiss on her lips. It was quick, just a taste of more to come. Yearning for more, he pulled away, breaking their embrace.

"We have plenty of time. Have a good night." Turning away, he sauntered over to his SUV and jumped into the driver's seat. Sophia stood, as if in a trance as she watched him pull out onto the dark street. *What on Earth was that?* Slowly, she chirped open her car with the remote door opener and just sat for a moment, waiting her heart rate to return to normal. Sophia would have been the happiest woman alive had she not just realized that Trent hadn't asked for her number.

Chapter Four

The Thursday before Valentine's Day

The weeks had melted together, Trent and Sophia growing closer with each passing day. Trent had wanted to take it slowly, he had told Sophia, so it wasn't until the third class that he had asked for her phone number. Sophia had seen him exactly twice outside of their cooking class but they texted or spoke on the phone most days. Trent informed her he had a very busy schedule, but she sensed that it was perhaps something more. Trent had been through something, he was guarded, mysterious, even. Tonight was the last class and Sophia was sweating out her plan. Despite the numerous cooking classes, she hadn't improved upon her cooking skills at all. The "final exam" as it was called, consisted of baking in front of the entire class. Trent had stated repeatedly that he loved a woman who could cook. And why would she ever admit that she burned toast? Sophia was horrified when he suggested that they make Valentine's Day cookies. The only thing she was good at was making a superb chocolate martini. That certainly wouldn't cut the mustard, so to speak.

Susan had been appalled when her twin had suggested "making the switch" just as they had done numerous times in their early years, fooling not only their teachers and friends, but their parents as well.

"There is no way!" Susan's voice boomed.

"But please, then you can go off for the weekend with what's his name and have a great time. Just do this one little thing for me." Sophia would get down on her knees and beg if necessary.

After almost half an hour of badgering her sister and following her around the apartment, Susan finally resolved to do her sister this favor.

"Fine, But I'm warning you that he's going to be mad. It's never a good idea to start off a relationship with a lie."

Waving her hands to the side, Sophia pushed the thought aside and then grabbed for her sister, wrapping her in a thankful hug. It was simple, Susan would do the baking, slip into the bathroom when finished, and then Sophia would appear in the same exact clothing and then-bam—mission accomplished.

***

Trent had looked forward to this all day. He could feel it in his bones; it was going to be a special night. The beautiful red roses that had purchased from the florist after work were on the kitchen table. He would wait until after they had prepared the Valentine's Day cookies for the class and then surprise her in front of everyone with the dozen roses and a kiss. *Women liked that kind of thing,* he thought and it excited him to think about how happy Sophia would be. Tonight would be the night to open up to Sophia also. He wanted to spend Valentine's Day with this woman and had secured reservations for the following night at the best Italian restaurant in the county. Feeling a twinge of excitement, he headed out the door, feeling that this was going to be a night he would not forget.

***

Sophia was running late tonight, he noticed as he glanced at the time on his cell. She had promised to bring all of the ingredients. Where was she? Half expecting her to rush though the door just like she did that very first night of cooking class, he kept his eyes peeled on the door. Minutes later, she walked in, cool as a cucumber. Being more than ten minutes late, he was surprised at how calm she appeared. Watching her gaze around the room, he wondered what was taking her so long to sit beside him.

"Sophia, let's go, we're up next." He gestured for her to join him at the table. An odd flash of recognition

19

registered on her face as she smiled and politely said hello to him. *Why was she being so proper all of a sudden?* Keeping his eyes straight ahead, he reached for Sophia's hand under the table as they watched the older couple prepare a veal parmesan entrée that filled the air with a delightful scent. Sophia jolted and practically leaped out of her chair at his touch.

"I'm sorry. Is everything okay?" His feelings stung a bit. Sophia glanced at him, clearing her throat.

"I'm fine, Trent." She whispered softly, eyes straight ahead.

It was hands off for the remainder of the class until it was their time to shine. With the expert touch of a chef, he watched in delight as Sophia seamlessly prepared their workstation for preparation of their cookies. She ordered him to pass her this and that, a real natural at this. He recalled how she had never seemed so confident about her abilities in class before, but, hey, who was he to complain? Together, they worked side by side, as they mixed the sugar, flour, water and other ingredients into the mixing bowl. They rolled the dough, cut out the heart shapes, sprinkled the sparkly red bits on top of each delectable cookie, and popped them in the oven. "Voila!" Sophia announced, dusting off her hands and taking a bow as the others clapped in admiration. "And just wait until you taste them!"

This overly confident woman seemed to have hidden the humble, chatty woman he knew. Spying Jackie, he followed her gaze to Sophia's face, noting the creased brows as Jackie sized her up and down. It appeared that Jackie noticed something was off about Sophia tonight as well.

"Excuse me a moment. I forgot to get my camera. Be right back." Jackie rushed out the door. This was the moment he had been waiting for. Excusing himself, he grabbed his jacket from across the room and reached for the red roses. His pulse raced as he walked closer to Sophia, taking his hand from behind his back to offer the roses to her. Her eyes went wide as she grasped the flowers, an unreadable expression plastered all over her face. He grabbed her and planted a kiss right on her lips. Unlike the other warm, emotional kisses they had shared, this one was tense, cold.

"Hey! Look who I've got here!" Jackie's voice boomed across the room, breaking off the frigid kiss. Standing right next to Jackie was none other than Sophia, with her hands twisting and a frown splayed across her face.

Trent released the woman whom he had baked with, the one he had given the flowers to and had kissed. "What is going on here?" His voice came across as a shocked whisper and somewhere in the back of his mind, he recalled Sophia telling him that she had a twin, an identical twin. But she had been fooling him all along, lying to him, giving him false hope... Bounding out of the room, he saw red. The real Sophia grasped his arm, begging him to listen.

"Get away from me." He shrugged her off with force, striding past her in a whirlwind of emotion. Anger, disappointment, embarrassment, regret.

He didn't acknowledge Jason's voice as he raced for the door and into his SUV.

***

Embarrassed, shamed, humiliated didn't even begin to describe how he felt. Susan was right; she should have been upfront and honest with Trent from the start. No, she couldn't cook, and no, she had no desire to learn, but she hadn't wanted to disappoint him.

Hours crawled by and finally Susan came home, most likely spending time with her own boyfriend. After a few minutes of comfort, her sister was off to pack for her weekend Valentine's Day trip. Recalling how she had been busted caused fresh tears to fall. Jackie had been shocked then angered by her betrayal, just like Trent had been.

There was the faint sound of a knock on the door, but who would it be at this hour? Wiping her tear stained face, Sophia reached for the door. Her eyes went wide as she spied Trent, a small grin playing on his smooth lips. Kindness crinkled his warm eyes and he grabbed her into his arms.

"You fool," he lectured after releasing her from his kiss. "Do you really thing that I would care that you couldn't cook?"

"But you told me how important it was to you, to have a woman who could stir up delicious meals…"

Tugging at her hair, Trent leaned in and rewarded Sophia with another deep kiss. "Your sister said that the only thing you can whip up is a delicious chocolate martini."

So that's where Susan had been, she must have gone after him, talking to Trent, trying to get him to understand why she had deceived him. Feeling that special spark that only twins can, Sophia turned knowing already that her sister was watching from the hallway with a twinkle in her eyes.

"So, do you want to try my chocolate martini?" Sophia teased.

"I'd rather you be my Valentine." Trent confessed as he kissed the tip of Sophia's nose.

"Oh, I think I can handle that." Sophia announced as she turned her head to look back at her sister. Susan tiptoed off down the hallway. When her twin was completely out of sight, Sophia grabbed Trent's collar and rewarded him with a kiss far sweeter than Valentine's Day cookies or even that chocolate martini.

"Now *that's* the way to my heart." Trent whispered.

Valentine's Day Recipes:

1. Susan's Valentine's Day Cookies:
Ingredients: Makes 4 dozen

7 cups all-purpose flour
2 cups white sugar
2 teaspoons salt
2 teaspoons baking powder
1 1/2 cups shortening
3 teaspoons vanilla extract
1 cup milk
3 eggs

Preheat oven to 375 degrees F
In a large mixing bowl, mix flour, sugar, salt, and baking powder together. Mix in shortening. Once the shortening is well blended, stir vanilla extract and milk into the dough, followed by eggs. Roll out dough onto a floured surface, using a floured rolling pin. Roll the dough thick. Cut out cookies using heart-shaped cutter and arrange them on a cookie sheet.
Bake at 375 degrees F for 8 to 10 minutes. Enjoy!

2. Sophia's Chocolate Martini:

1 1/2 ounces chocolate liqueur
1 1/2 ounces crème de cacao
1/2 ounce vanilla vodka
1/2 ounces half and half
Chocolate syrup for rim

Mix all ingredients in a cocktail shaker filled with ice and shake well.

Pour into a chilled cocktail glass that is rimmed with chocolate syrup.

Yum!

Him & Her
Rocky Rochford

Chapter One
Him

I had watched her my entire life, ever since she and her family moved to the Carlisle Industrial Estate in the city of London. Now that I said that out loud, I realised that sounded a little creep.

If not very creepy.

But I didn't mean it like that.

From the day we met, we soon became friends. She knows nearly everything there is to know about me, as I do her and yet, despite how much I have always wanted something to happen, but it never did and I'm starting to think it never will.

God, I sound like a right downer.

No wonder I'm still single.

My name is Donny Tyler and I am an eighteen-year-old, London lad, born and raised in the Carlisle Estate. This wasn't just the world I was brought up in, but the only one I have ever known, but she's the one who makes it all worthwhile.

Chapter Two
Her

He thinks I didn't, but I caught him looking at me again today. It's always the same way, the same gentle fondness and gentle glint he always has.

I knew he harbored feelings for me, I'd be a fool not to, but every time it's like he might actually get there and ask me out, or say something about it, the words just refuse to come.

It wasn't so long ago that I used to spend my days wanting nothing more than to have lips part and words form, but there is only so long you can spend waiting on someone to say something before it comes to a time you have to move on. As cruel as that sounds.

Sure I could have done the talking for him, to tell him that I feel exactly the same way. This was urban London, after all, and the 21st century.

Despite being the 'hard as nails, show me attitude, I'll show you some right back,' type of girl I am, at the end of the day I still want my Disney ending. That one guy who comes along and sweeps me off my feet right at the end, after the big song and dance.

I hope you don't hold that against me.

Looking down at the ground far below, I could see a couple of the estate's younger kids kicking a ball around. Off to the right were the hooded older kids, who only a few years ago, were the younger kids kicking the ball around.

To my right I heard approaching footsteps. I looked up and saw *him*.

Get ready for an awkward moment.

Chapter Three
Him

*J*anie's blue eyes were staring in my direction, focused right on me, I wasn't intentionally trying to walk in her direction, but here I am.

It would be rude if I didn't say anything, so I stopped alongside.

"Hey, Janie, you all right?" I asked.

She shrugged her shoulders and put her hands in her jacket pockets.

"Yeah, I'm decent, Donny, you?"

"Ah, you know."

I bobbed my head a bit. There was no denying things had become awkward between us the last couple of days.

"Yeah," was all she said.

Just staring into those blue eyes of hers was enough to give me butterflies and start thinking about what dating her could be like.

"You still there, Donny?" she asked, easily recognizing the distant look my eyes made whenever I zoned out.

Why can't I just ask her out?

Why do I always keep losing my nerve?

Then I remembered she's seeing someone.

And that's why I don't ask.

Because there is always someone else.

"Yeah I'm still here," I finally replied.

"You must have been thinking about something good, you were smiling," she remarked.

"Ah, just this and that," I immediately replied.

No way in Hell was I going to be honest.

"So how's things with Derek going?"

Derek was obviously the latest guy in her life.

Janie's faced turned to disgust before it eased up a little.

"Well, between Derek and *Charlene* things are going very well," she said.

I was a little lost and for Janie, my face was all too easy to read.

"He was cheating on me with a girl from college," she explained.

"Ah," I said.

That's it. "Ah," that's really all I could say. I'm an idiot.

"It's not your fault, you didn't know."

"Yeah but still. You shouldn't keep being done over like you are," I said.

"It's fine, he's only the third guy in a month. It's just the way things go, one minute you're born and the next it's all downhill."

Janie always did have a way of putting on a brave face.

"Yeah."

"So what about you, have you got a girl yet? Or anyone you've got your eye on?"

I don't know why, but right as she asked that, I couldn't tell if she was just asking out of interest, or if she was fishing.

"Nah, you know me," I remarked.

She laughed.

"That I do, but I'm sure you'll find someone, some time. You're an all right bloke, I guess."

This time, I laughed, only to have my brow arch. There was something about the way she said it.

Was she being coy?

Was she coming onto me?

"And you're not too bad on the eye, I suppose. I'm sure you'll find a nice guy sooner or later." I responded.

Was I flirting with her just then?

I think I was.

That's new.

"Yeah maybe, but my trouble is, I could look him in the eye every day, passing him as I go on about my day and that would be it. Nothing more."

If she wasn't coming onto me before, she definitely was then.

This is it, Donny. That right moment you have been waiting for your entire life for. Say it. Ask her out right now.

I went to open my mouth, but nothing came.

She looked at me, as if waiting.

Come on Donny, this is it. You can do it.

Still nothing.

For the love of God, just do it! I screamed to myself, but still I just couldn't do it, just like always. Janie looked disappointed with my lack of speaking.

"Silly me, I've got stuff to do," she said.

"Yeah, yeah, of course, me too," I replied.

And things are just getting more and more awkward.

"So er, I'll be seeing you around."

"I'll be right here," I shot back.

"I'll be right here," you dopey idiot.

Janie started to walk away.

You see that, she's leaving and so is your last chance to ever ask her, I implored to myself.

But it was to no avail, I still couldn't say anything.

She's going to Donny, going...

Janie took some more steps, not looking back.

...Going...

The distance was getting even bigger.

"Hey, Janie!" I cried.

Where did that come from?

"What?" She snapped, turning round.

If you're really going to do this, Donny, you do it and you do it right now. No more thinking about it, make it happen.

I marched right over to her.

Do it, Donny!

"There's been something I've been meaning to ask you," I said. I don't know how I got the words out, but I did.

"And what's that?" she asked, putting her hands on her hips.

Now, Donny, do it now!

"I like you, I always have. Do you want to get dinner some time?"

Holy Hell, I actually asked her.

My words shocked us both, but she soon quickly smiled and looked me right in the eye.

"You mean like a date?" she probed.

You're doing good, Donny, I told myself reassuringly.

"Exactly like a date," I answered.

She smiled approvingly.

"Donny, I have been waiting for you to ask for a long time." Her words were unexpected.

"You were?"

"Yep."

I wanted to kick myself. Now that this was actually happening, I could see that this was so much more easier than I ever thought.

"You serious about this, Donny?"

Don't blow it now, mate.

"Yeah, I am," I answered with a confidence I never knew I had.

"Good. You can pick me up tonight at seven."

Janie leaned up and kissed me on the cheek before she headed for home.

Chapter Four
Her

*N*ever in a million years did I actually think he'd do it, that he'd actually get round to asking, and yet he did.

I guess some people are capable of change after all.

Sure it could all go horribly wrong, but after three years of waiting, in the twelve that I have known him, I owe it to the both of us to try it at least.

So I sat at home, wasting the few short hours before the time of our date, thinking up the million and one ways this evening could play out.

I wished I could say that at least half of the million were good ways for it to go, but I'd be lying. It is always so easy to get so focused on only the bad. I was getting so antsy

Thank God, I picked tonight and not tomorrow.

But time just ticked right on by and before I knew it, it was six thirty already, so I grabbed a quick shower and picked out something nice, as opposed to something slutty I usually wear for my dates with jerks, and I sat by the front door in wait. Doubt came creeping in.

He's not coming, he's going to cancel at the last second. I began to think.

I looked at the analogue watch on my wrist.

18:59.

He's not coming, he's cancelled.

I looked again, it's still 18:59.

He's not coming. I repeated.

My watch struck 19:00 and just as I was about to think some more doubt, there was a knock on my door.

I guess he didn't cancel.

Times really were changing.

Chapter Five
Him

She opened the door, just as I was quarrelling with myself that I'd made a mistake by turning up right on time, when the truth was I've been stood out here in my leather jacket and jeans for the last ten minutes.

My eyes fell upon her and I was breathless.

She looked like a goddess.

So beautiful and everything I ever wanted in a single package.

"You realise this is the part where you're supposed to say something about how I look?" she playfully remarked.

It took me a couple of seconds, but I was able to say one thing.

"You look gorgeous."

Chapter Six
Her

*D*onny's eyes were wide with admiration and as for his comment, I knew he meant it. I cast my own gaze over his appearance. He was wearing the jacket I bought him during our last year at school. He bought us our first legal pints in that jacket.

He also had on his favourite faded pair of jeans and had his wild hair tamed for once. He didn't look too bad himself.

"You scrub up pretty well yourself," I said. The words were enough to bring a smile to his face.

I always did love his smile.

The way it was just lights up the room.

"So dinner huh, we are we going?" I asked, as it hadn't been mentioned once. "And as a classy girl, you know I require the best.

"Funny," he chuckled.

His eyes beamed kindly.

I don't know what it was about him, but he seemed so much more different than his usual self. He was so much more confident

The difference a single question can make.

"But seriously though, I think you might like what I've got planned. I can guarantee you that you have never had a date like this one before," he said and you know what? I believed him.

I left behind my flat and followed him out to the landing. I placed my arm in his as we walked anxiously over to the stairs.

Out of habit, I thought we'd be heading down, to the world below where cars are parked and restaurants existed where every day people go to eat and drink, but we didn't.

"Not that way," he said as he began to lead me upstairs.

"What are you up to?" I asked, slightly unsure.

"Just trust me," he said.

If this was anyone else, I'd have walked away there and then, but it wasn't anyone else.

It was Donny Tyler.

"Ok," I answered. The two of us headed up the stairs, going all the way to the highest floor and further. Not even the locked door to stop people from actually getting out and being on the roof could stop us as Donny produced a key from his pocket and unlocked the door.

"Since when do you have a key to the roof?" I asked, interested.

"Since I started helping Mr. Johnson feed his pet pigeons from time to time," he answered.

"His pigeons?"

I felt slightly alarmed. Ever since I was a child, I had a fear of birds, silly I know, but there you go. Just one of those things, I guess.

"Don't worry, they're kept in a cage and are nicely secured. They won't be bothering us tonight, besides the occasional cooing," he explained.

"If you say so," I remarked.

Waiting no longer, he pushed the door open and walked out. I quickly followed behind him.

"So what do you think?" he asked, indicating all that was around us.

First my eyes fell onto the camping stove that was already set up. Then to the blankets laid out on the floor and a telescope that was set up and aimed at the few visible stars above. Lastly there was the view itself, the view of the city I'd come to love, all light up in the dark at night.

Donny had done all of this for me. I was speechless.

Chapter Seven
Him

There I was with my arms outstretched, sharing with the girl I always fancied, everything I had arranged for our perfect night, and she stood before me not saying anything at all.

Immediately, I began to worry.

Oh God, she hates it. She really hates it.

It felt like all of eternity itself had passed before she finally spoke.

"It's the nicest thing anyone has ever done for me," she confessed.

Relief took over.

"Yeah, well, it gets better." I walked over the CD player I had hidden and hit play. Immediately an old favorite of ours began to play. She smiled in recognition.

"That's not..."

"It sure is," I answered.

"I thought your disk broke ages ago," she countered.

"Oh it did, I brought this especially for today."

Before I gave her the chance to say anything more, an all too familiar line began to play. I couldn't help but sing along for old time's sake.

Neither could she.

Not only did the two of us sing along to the chorus, but we sang the entire song and the one that followed. Sure we could do the typical first time date and talk about stuff, but the thing is, we've been talking our entire lives. Just being in this moment and making it the best experience either one of us have ever had was what tonight was all about.

Chapter Eight
Her

*N*ever before had any of my dates ever been this easy, the two of us just so easily clicking into place, as we sang our hearts out. Sure we were terrible and off-key, but it really didn't matter.

I guess we were just so in touch with the moment.

When the moment did pass and the duet finished, I soon turned my sights to the telescope itself.

"So what's with the telescope then? A little toy you like to use whenever you're up here to perve on the occasional passing girl," I jested.

"Hilarious, but no. Actually it's for this."

Donny motioned for me to stroll over and take a look, so I did. He just so happened to have it set up on one of my all-time favourite constellations that was visible this time of year.

"For as long as I've known you, you've always been interested in astronomy," he whispered into my ear.

Nicely played Donny.
Nicely done indeed.

I moved away from the telescope and looked to the blankets.

"And what are they for, dare I ask? You predicting some snuggling?"

"Not at all. I just merely thought in case it got too cold, we could easily warm up. That and be able to lie down and just gaze upwards," he shot back, his confidence still holding.

In all the time I have known him, I've never seen this side to him.

"Oh." I acted downhearted. "And I was so looking forwards to snuggling."

"Well, no need to rule anything out just yet," he flirted in reply.

"I'll have to try it out first though," I retorted before I lay down on the blankets.

Even without the cushions, I thought it was incredibly comfy.

"Hmm, nope, no good at all. I'm going to need a second opinion." I patted the spot directly in front of him, calling him over.

Despite everything that had already happened and his new confidence, I never actually expected him to walk over and lay down beside me, but he did.

Our faces were so close together. My eyes looked into his and his into mine.

"You're right, this is no good at all," he answered.

"Maybe this will make things more comfortable."

Donny had already done the most of the work; this was the least I could do. I leaned forwards and planted my lips on his. At first, it was like a small peck, as he pulled away, as if unnerved, only to return and lean into me, taking control of the kiss.

Our lips stayed together for what felt like all of time and just like everything else up until now, it was perfect. It was what I always dreamed of, but had always been denied.

With lips apart, we stared at one another. Neither of us wanted to break the silence, but break it I would.

"So what about this dinner then, or did you lead me up here under false pretences?"

"Not at all, but after that, it's going to be hard to beat," he replied with a coy smile.

"Well then, I guess you're just going to have to try."

Chapter Nine
Him

She's talking about me making a start on dinner, while I'm still reeling from being blown away by that kiss. Well, I guess I best get to it.

I wouldn't want to blow all my hard work now.

"Your wish is my command, but you stay right there."

"Cross my heart," she said, as she quite literally crossed her heart.

I got up and moved over to the camp stove. With the first match, it lit easily and I continued where I had left off. Haven chosen to make a simple carbonara, I had already precooked the pasta and the pre-seasoned mushrooms and bacon before I added it altogether in the big pot. All that was really required to do was heat it all together and make the creamy cheese sauce to go with it.

As the remaining water I kept from when I boiled the pasta earlier started to boil, I quickly added the egg yolk I whisked previously and the parmesan cheese. I'm not really a fan of cheese myself, but Janie certainly was, so I added a fair amount and poured in some milk.

Janie lay on the blanket watching me. Interested in just what I was cooking up, she walked over to me and inspected it.(ok)

"Ah, spaghetti carbonara I see," she said approvingly.

Of course she did, it was her favorite after all.

"I seem to recall someone having a penchant for cheesy meals." I replied, as I stirred the entire contents in the saucepan. Dinner would be in mere minutes.

"You're quite far ahead, close to dishing up." She shot me a look. "You already prepared this before I got here didn't you?"

"I just thought it would save some time, time we could put to good use by doing other things."

"What kind of other things?" She smiled demurely.

"Oh, I don't know, I thought I'd let you decide."

I moved my gaze from her and added my last touch of seasoning, just a little more garlic, oregano, and mixed herbs. I gave it all a minute to mix in before I turned the gas off and looked at her.

"Dinner is ready."

Janie clapped her hands excitedly.

"Why don't you go sit down and I'll dish it up and bring it over to you?" I offered.

"I suppose I could."

I watched her walk away and sit down on the blanket, the playful glint in her eye a sure sign to me that she approved of how everything was going.

My hands reached for plates as I dished up our meal, rather generous helpings, I'll add, but I was sure we'd be able to eat it and then afterwards we had cornettos for desert.

Before I gave Janie her plate, I made sure to sprinkle just a touch more cheese on top, just in case it wasn't enough before. I walked over to join her, carrying our dinner and cutlery.

She looked at me as if this was the start of something neither of us had ever had before.

I knew the date wasn't over yet, but given the way it was going, I just couldn't help but ask a question, as I placed her plate in front of her and sat down opposite.

"So what do you reckon, Janie, will there be a second date?"

"I don't know," she laughed. "I guess it determines on what this tastes like."

She took her fork and brought a small mouthful to her mouth.

I knew her answer before she even said it. The kiss had already said it all.

Spaghetti Carbonara Recipe:

The basic recipe that can be used to feed between two to as many people you want and is open to altering by changing of ingredients, in the event of the required ingredient not being available.

Usually takes between 15-20 minutes.

Ingredients:

*Around 200g of spaghetti (or linguine if you prefer) for a decent serving, for two people (add more, for more people)

*Diced pancetta, or in the event of no pancetta, it can be replaced with either streaky bacon, ham, and cut up wieners, depending on what you have at the time. (Around 100g would do for a serving of two, but depending on the quantity of guests and the appetite of those who will be eating the meal, you will want to add more.)

*Chopped mushrooms, either fresh or canned and the quantity depends really on your own personal preference

*2 tsp olive oil

*1 garlic clove, crushed, or even garlic powder will do

*1 pinch of salt

*3 pinches of oregano

*2 pinches of mixed herbs

*1 egg

*50g of either grated parmesan, or failing that, any type of cream cheese, including cheese-spreads.

*A pouring of milk (this just purely depends on preference)

How it's Done: The Prep Work

-If using fresh mushrooms, now is a good time to chop them up, followed by the pancetta, bacon or whatever meat you have chosen to use.

How it's Done: The Cooking

Put the spaghetti (or linguine) in the saucepan and start to boil it.

Get the frying pan on and add some olive oil so you can begin to fry your chosen meat, on a moderate heat.

Monitor both as they cook and add your mushrooms in with your meat, and throw in your garlic, a pinch of mixed herbs and oregano.

When your spaghetti is close to cooked, pour out most of the water and put the spaghetti and remaining water into a new pan, large enough for everything to fit in to.

Now the mushrooms and meat should be done and able to be taken off and added to the pasta.

Mix it all in and get your egg out. Carefully break the shell and whisk the egg yolk before also adding it to the pan with everything in.

This is the part where the creamy sauce gets made. With the egg already in, you add your milk and your preferred type of cheese before adding that pinch of salt and remaining oregano and mixed herbs.

With everything in the pot, gently mix it all in and stir continuously until the creamy sauce meets your preference. The longer you simmer it for, the sauce will get thin, so if you want a thick creamy sauce, remove sooner. If a thinner sauce to completely soaked into every ingredient ~~side,~~ is what you're after than that's what you do.

Once the carbonara to how you like it, you can dish it up and add a little more cheese, sprinkled at the table before you can sit down and enjoy.

And that is just one of many ways to make a cheesy Spaghetti Carbonara.

There's Always Tomorrow
Susanne Matthews

*D*ressed in a strapless black silk gown that fell loosely from her bust hiding the orthopedic shoes and the metal braces she wore on her legs, Iris waited for Pete to pull out the chair so she could sit. She'd made it from the entrance to the table using her brother-in-law's arm rather than her walker, and now she stood with a death grip on the edge of the white, linen-covered table, hoping her legs would hold her up just a few moments longer.

She could feel the eyes of the curious boring into her back. Did they recall Fleur, the former face of Avalon Cosmetics, or did they see remnants of shy, little Iris Taylor, the girl who'd been afraid of her own shadow? Why had she ever let her sisters convince her to leave her sanctuary and attend this dinner?

As if I really had a choice. They'd have dragged me here kicking and screaming tonight if I'd refused. One night. I can do this for one night.

"Relax, Iris," Lily said settling into the chair one over from hers and reaching over to pat her hand reassuringly. "Smile. You look fine. The plastic surgeon did an excellent job. If anything's going to make people look at you twice, it's that "deer in the headlights" look on your face. These people are friends and family. No one's going to say or do anything to hurt you."

"I just feel as if they're all gawking at me…"

"No, they aren't. Look around. Everyone is busy greeting one another. They may have glanced up when we entered, but I'm sure my whale-like proportions garnered more interest than you did. That didn't come out right." She shook her head and smiled. "Of course they noticed you. You're just as stunning as you always were, way too thin, but once you start getting out and eating more… Thanks, honey," she added to her husband as he pushed her chair in as close to the table as her pregnant belly would allow.

Pete turned to help her. "Thanks," Iris said, settling onto the chair and praying she could get through the meal and the rest of the evening without having to make a trip to the ladies' room. The thought of having to ask for an escort was enough to ensure her bowels and bladder took a six-hour break.

"Would you care for a cocktail?" the waiter asked.

"I'd like a glass of wine, but club soda with lime will have to do," Lily answered.

"The same for me, please," Iris said softly.

"Hey, I'm the one on the wagon thanks to the twins." Lily said rubbing her stomach.

"I'm fine. I'll have something with dinner," she fibbed. She'd love a glass of wine, a little liquid courage to help her through this, but didn't dare indulge herself. What if the wine affected her balance? She was like Bambi on ice as it was, and the more tired she got, the worse it would be.

She took a sip from the water glass in front of her and turned back to her sister. "I heard you decided to keep the family tradition after all. What changed your mind?"

"Mom. It seems every Gardner girl has been named after a plant or a flower for more than a hundred years, and my suggestion to end it was met with tears and the guilt trip from hell. Pete sided with her, saying traditions are important, so I gave in gracefully. Rose has her Heather, and we'll have Holly and Ivy. That doesn't leave too many decent choices for you."

"I doubt that'll be a problem. Unless I'm looking at the next Immaculate Conception, I'm not going to be in the position to be picking out names."

The thought sobered her. Freezing rain and a drunk driver had stolen everything she'd ever wanted from her two years ago—her face, her husband, and her dreams of a family of her own. Models with damaged faces who could barely walk weren't well suited to the life. Her agent had apologized, but there was nothing he could do. At least the insurance company hadn't balked at paying out the two million dollar policy she'd taken out on her career three years ago, after that Italian model had acid thrown in her face by some stalker.

"Darling, you look wonderful," her mother gushed as she approached the table. "I love your hair like that. I always said it looked better short." She bent and kissed her on both cheeks. "I'm so glad you finally decided to get out of that house and join the human race again."

"Mom, I've only been back six weeks. It's not like I'm alone there all the time. Rose and Lily call or drop by almost every day."

"I know, you've got a housekeeper and a physiotherapist too, but you need to be with people, darling. Now that you're settled and have left your self-imposed prison, I'm sure you'll have all kinds of invitations to get out again. People were just waiting for you to be ready."

"Mom's right," Lily added. "Lara's been begging me to ask you to attend Career Day at the high school."

"Whatever for?" she asked, surprised that anyone would think she had anything to offer.

"You're still a celebrity with lots of experience. You'd be an invaluable resource," her mother stated baldly, and Iris smiled uncomfortably at her, praying she was wrong.

The last thing she wanted was to become the social center of Harper. People meant well, but... Fleur was a persona she'd worn, not who she'd been, and as much as she hated what had happened to her, she didn't miss her modeling career. She was really an introvert. Hosting all those dinners for Howard's friends had been difficult, especially at the end when their marriage might as well have been over. If he hadn't been killed, they'd have divorced. She was quite content to be in the shadows, left alone to her own devices—lonely, hell yes, but that was the price she paid for her anonymity. There was only one man she'd ever really wanted, and he was as far out of her reach now as he'd ever been.

"We'll see, Mom. One day at a time." She turned as her dad approached, and blinked her eyes to hold back the tears. She'd always been a daddy's girl, and while her mother sometimes intimidated her, Dad was her best friend.

"Hello, princess."

She longed to stand and fling herself into his arms, but that wasn't going to happen. Instead, she hugged him fiercely as he bent to kiss her.

"Hi, Daddy. You're looking great. The West Coast weather seems to agree with you."

"You're welcome to come and stay with us anytime, Iris," her mother said. "The climate would be so much better for you. Even if you insisted on having your own place, there are lots of condos and houses available in Victoria. Staying in that drafty old mausoleum isn't healthy. I never liked it even when I lived there."

"Now, Marguerite, cut the girl some slack. We agreed not to talk about this tonight, remember?"

"Fine, but she should get away from here and start over."

Iris breathed a sigh of relief as Mom moved on to Lily, and then sat next to Pete.

"I wonder what's keeping the woman of the hour," Lily said, changing the topic and nervously reaching up to push a lock of her silver blonde hair behind her ears, allowing her gold and silver chandelier earring to dangle freely. "I'd have expected the new Justice of the Peace to be here already."

"She's here," Frank said, coming over to join them at the table. "Rose is in the back with the other three new justices. We arrived almost an hour ago. I've never seen her so excited." He looked every inch as proud of his wife as they all were. Bending, he kissed Lily on the cheek and patted her tummy. "Hello, ladies. How much longer?"

"Any day now," Lily answered and chuckled. "I feel ready to pop."

"They'll be no popping tonight," Pete said, reaching for his wife's hand.

"I certainly hope not," said her father. "We're planning to stick around until the babies arrive. No need to do everything in one day."

Lily giggled and rubbed her belly. "Hear that, girls? Daddy and Grandpa agree. You need to stay put for a couple more days."

"Let's hope they listen better than Owen does," Pete said with a laugh. "Lately our son has disagreed with whatever we tell him to do."

I hope so too. The last place she wanted to end up tonight was in the hospital. She'd spent far too much time there in the last two years as it was.

Frank sat in the chair on her left and reached over to kiss her cheek. "You know, having you here tonight has made Rose's evening. You look great."

"You don't look so bad yourself in that penguin suit, Doc," she said. "The last time I saw you in a tuxedo was at my wedding five years ago." The memories of that day were bittersweet, but she wouldn't give in to melancholy.

"A country vet doesn't get to dress up much, but seeing you here tonight has made my supreme sacrifice worth it." He rubbed his index finger between his neck and his collar. "I watched you walk in. I'm impressed. You've made great progress. Pretty soon you'll be running again."

The waiter arrived with their drinks and Iris took the opportunity to glance around the hotel ballroom. The decorations sparkled in the subdued light. A giant black and silver gavel, its hammer section filled with glitter, hung high at the front above the dais, the symbol of the new careers the four guests of honor were embarking on. In the far corner, a small string quartet played softly. Lily had said they'd be replaced by a dance band after the meal. She loved dancing, but that was another pleasure she'd never enjoy again.

She sighed. *No pity party tonight. This is Rose's turn to shine.*

Glancing around the table, she realized it had been set for eight. Why eight? The only one missing was Rose. She was about to ask when she noticed Lily nervously folding and unfolding her napkin, glancing at the door. *They wouldn't dare!* You'd think that, after all these years, she'd have learned to recognize her sisters' matchmaking, but this was too much. They'd fixed her up with someone, she was sure of it, and it was that and not the prospect of premature labor that had Lily on pins and needles.

"You didn't," she whispered between clenched teeth, and Lily shrugged.

"It was Rose's idea..."

"Hello, Iris," a man's voice, one she'd heard countless times in interviews she'd taped and replayed, one that had always made her heart beat faster, interrupted her sister's comment. Lily blew out a deep breath and reached for her glass.

Iris's stunned gaze rose to meet chocolate brown eyes filled with humor staring down at her, and her mouth gaped open. *This can't be real.*

His mouth twitched as he tried not to smile, but his dimple gave it away. She hadn't seen Finn Bowman in person in more than fifteen years, not since he'd left Harper High on an athletic scholarship to Queen's. She knew he'd made it to the CFL, she'd watched him play on television, had even attended the Grey Cup the year his team had won, but she'd lost track of him and so many other things in life these last couple of years.

Slowly her brain started to function again. "Finn. This is a surprise. What are you doing here? You look great. Are you still playing for the Lions? I didn't know you were in town." She was blabbering like the shy sophomore she'd been, the one who'd have gladly died for one on Finn's smiles. The crush she'd had on him had been painful, but he'd been nineteen to her fifteen, and she'd known nothing would come from her unrequited love.

"I had to retire three years ago—busted my knee too badly to keep playing if I wanted to walk. I've been back here since. I guess your sisters forgot to mention I was your date for this shindig. Sorry about that. I hope you aren't too disappointed—I'm not." He smiled at the others seated at the table. "Where's Rosie?"

Frank chuckled. "You know you're the only man on earth who gets away with calling her that? She's out back with the others. They're going to pipe them in shortly." He took a mouthful of beer. "By the way, she said to tell you it's tomorrow, whatever that means."

"Old joke," Finn said, and worked his way around the table, shaking hands with the other members of her family and a few strangers who approached him.

Iris's eyes were glued on the man who'd been the object of her girlish fantasies. He looked good—too damn good. She'd always been a sucker for a man in a tux. Time had treated him kindly. The gangling youth she remembered from high school was now a well-muscled man, but as a pro quarterback, he'd have to be in shape, and he'd obviously kept it up. His chestnut hair was cut short and sprinkled with strands of silver. He sat down beside her and the warmth in his eyes helped her relax. If she had to have an escort tonight, she couldn't think of anyone she'd prefer. Being with him was a girlish dream come true. She just might forgive Rose and Lily after all.

The whine of the bagpipes brought the buzz of

conversation to a halt, and the crowd stood. Iris sat still, glued to her chair. Standing would take a lot of effort and people would notice—he'd notice. So much for her magical evening. Her heart beat faster and her palms sweated as she tried to push the chair away from the table to stand.

"Let me help you," whispered Finn, pulling the chair out and putting his arm around her, lifting her upright quickly, and keeping his arm there as if she were too precious to release.

Iris swallowed the tears of gratitude clogging her throat, and clung to her knight in tuxedoed armor. The piper entered the room followed by the mayor, the minister of the local Presbyterian Church, and the two new justices, each wearing their black robes of office. The piper climbed the two steps to the stage and moved over to the side. The party stopped at center stage and the mayor stepped up to the podium.

"Ladies and gentleman," he said as soon as the last note faded. "It's my pleasure to introduce you to tonight's guests of honor. Madame Justice Rose Taylor Brown and Justice Ted Newcomb." The room burst into applause. "Now, if you'd please join in the singing of our national anthem, we can get the festivities underway. *O Canada, our home and native land...*" The mayor's rich baritone filled the room and the guests joined in. When the anthem was over, he spoke again. "Please remain standing as the Reverend Fred Mahoney leads us in prayer."

Finn had moved his arm down around her waist, but he hadn't released her. Normally she could stand under her own steam for a few minutes, and she was getting better at it all the time, but she was grateful for his support. As Reverend Mahoney intoned his prayer, she realized she felt less alone and exposed than she had half an hour ago. Finn had always made her feel safe. Maybe that was why she'd idolized him so much. More like worshipped. How many times had he come to her rescue when some creep or bully had been on her case? She'd gone from ugly duckling to swan almost overnight, but he'd never changed the way he treated her. To him, she'd been Rosie's kid sister, but to her, he'd been the be all and end all of her dreams.

"Amen." The word pulled her back to the present.

Finn settled her in the chair and handed her the napkin that had fallen to the floor. "I think these things should be lined with gripper tape. I can never keep mine on my lap."

"Gripper tape's a little extreme, don't you think? It might damage too many fine fabrics." *Seriously, Iris. That was a joke, relax.*

Rose came down from the stage and over to the table. "Thank you all so much for being here," she said, "I've waited a long time for us to be together like this."

"Don't exaggerate. We were together at Iris's in Toronto before Mom and Dad went back home," Lily said. "That was only three months ago."

Rose frowned. "You know what I mean—out together, the Gardner bouquet in bloom."

"I haven't heard that expression since high school," Finn said. "I always felt privileged to know each blossom personally. Thanks for inviting me, Rosie. You know what this means to me." While he might have been speaking to Rose, he was looking at her, and Iris felt her cheeks flush.

"Hey, as you always said, there's always tomorrow," Rose winked at him, and Finn laughed.

Iris was sure she'd missed something important, but table service began, and the waiter who'd brought their drinks placed a cream soup in front of them. Finn crinkled his nose at it, the way a child might if someone served him something he didn't like, and she suppressed a giggle.

"Don't look at it like that. I'm sure it's delicious. This place has the best food outside of Toronto."

"That may be, but when my mom gave me cream soup, it usually meant she'd cleaned out the fridge and put stuff in it I didn't like."

Her mother laughed. "And we thought it was a secret. I think all mothers do that, but in my case, it was the only way to get Reg to eat his vegetables."

"I eat vegetables," her dad said defensively.

"Sure you do, but none of the ones that are really good for you."

"Says you. I happen to think peas are an excellent vegetable."

"They are," Rose said, "but there are lots of other veggies out there, Dad."

"If you say so…"

Finn tasted the pale orange concoction before him. "This is good."

Rose chuckled. "Of course it's good. I got to set the menu. I chose this soup, knowing it was one of Iris's favorites—spiced pumpkin."

"I've heard of pumpkin pie, but pumpkin soup?"

Iris laughed for what she was sure was the first time in years. "People can make soup out of just about anything, Finn. I used to make a cauliflower and cheese soup Dad said was to die for."

"Well, I love cauliflower and cheese. When can I come to dinner?"

Iris looked at him, expecting to see the teasing humor on his face. Instead, she saw sincerity and an eagerness that astonished her.

"I don't make too many things from scratch these days," she said apologetically.

"Why not? You have to eat," he said, polishing off the rest of his soup as the others did. He lowered his voice to keep the conversation between them. "Aren't the cupboards and counters at the right level for you? I went by the measurements your dad gave me, but if they aren't right, I can fix them. It would only take a day or so."

"You're the one who renovated my grandmother's

house for me?"

"I did. There are still a few things I'd like to add, but you moved in before I could get to them. I was planning on coming to talk to you, and then Rosie called last week and asked me to round out the party tonight... Don't be too angry with her. She's been really worried about you—we all have."

"I'm not angry, surprised maybe that you'd be willing to give up your time for me. What about your wife or girlfriend..."

"If that's your way of asking if I'm free, the answer is I have no wife or girlfriend, at least not yet, but I'm hoping to change that in the near future. Now, what about those cupboards?"

Iris felt the heat burn her cheeks. "No, I didn't mean it like that, I..." She saw the muscle in his jaw tense as he fought not to laugh at her. "Damn you, Finn Bowman. Everything is fine. I just didn't realize you'd done the work. The bill was a lot less than I'd expected."

"I didn't charge for the labor. You can get a good size tax break on the materials."

Iris's jaw fell open and then snapped shut. It had taken several weeks and at least two hundred man-hours to get that house ready for her. Both bathrooms and the kitchen had been modernized. An elevator had been installed and there wasn't a nook or cranny inaccessible to her. Outside, the front walk had been reconfigured to take her to the side of the veranda where a lift moved her from street level to the first floor, all done without taking anything away from the picturesque façade of the Queen Anne styled house. At the back, a ramp led from the yard to the back veranda, and another gave her access to the in-ground pool. Everything had been done to make the place as handicapped accessible as possible, but she vowed she'd be able to walk and climb stairs under her own power again one day.

Conversation around the table grew general as the empty soup dishes were replaced by plates of Caesar salad.

"Red or white?" asked Finn as the waiter came to the table with the wine.

"Neither, thanks," she replied, noting the white was one of her favorite chardonnays.

"Don't you like wine?" he asked as the server filled his glass with white wine.

"I like it, but I don't want to take any chances tonight. The last thing I want to do is lose my balance and fall."

Finn leaned so close to her she could feel his breath tickle the fine hairs on her neck. "Red or white? What kind of an escort would I be if I let you fall?"

I've already fallen. Fifteen years ago, and now I'm down for the count.

"You don't have to do this," she whispered back.

"Do what?" His wrinkled forehead showed his confusion.

"This, be nice to me. Treat me as if this were anything but a pity date to help out an old friend."

She watched the muscle jump in his jaw and knew she'd annoyed him.

"Iris, get this straight. I'm not here because I pity you or because Rosie asked me to accompany you. I'm here because I want to be. You and I need to get some things cleared up and this is one of them. I'm exactly where I want to be with the woman I want to be with. Now, red or white?"

"White please," she said glancing around to see if everyone had been watching them and noting each person was absorbed in a conversation of their own.

Prime rib cooked to perfection served with whipped potatoes and mixed vegetables followed the salad. When the waiter came around with the wine again, Finn suggested they try the merlot, and she didn't argue, still too stunned by the intensity of his words to even consider doing so. *He wants to be here with me.* If midnight came, and all this turned into ashes, she'd crawl out if need be, but she'd enjoy every last second.

Finn was everything she'd ever dreamed of in a date. He was funny, making her laugh over and over again at some outrageous comments. He talked about his life as a Canadian pro football player, and the crazy things fans did to get his attention.

"You're serious, she mailed you her underwear?"

"She did, and believe me when I saw the size of them, I was glad I'd missed her at the stadium."

"You're mean," she said and chuckled. "I'm sure she has a wonderful personality."

"That may be, but I wasn't interested in her—in any of them."

She put down her fork, surprised to see she'd eaten her entire meal. "Do you miss it?"

"The game? Sometimes, but I don't miss the traveling or the beating I took on some days. I'm ready to settle down."

"Have you thought of coaching?" He'd make a terrific coach. He had tons of patience and he cared. Just look at the way he was treating her tonight.

"Funny you should ask. Principal Granger over at Harper High asked if I'd consider taking over as Offensive Coach."

"And…"

"And I said I'd think about it. More wine?"

She nodded, and he refilled her glass. The meal ended with a maple crème brulée and coffee, followed by the unofficial swearing in of the new justices and words of thanks from all of them. Rose would make a good Justice of the Peace. She'd be tough but fair.

When the speeches ended, the string quartet who'd entertained throughout the meal was replaced by the dance band. Conversation was difficult, but she sat back, enjoying the music and the feel of Finn's arm across her shoulders. The tempo changed and the other couples at the table got up to dance.

"It's their song." She indicated her parents as the orchestra began to play *It Had To Be You.*

"Dance with me," Finn said standing.

"I can't," she said looking at him, wishing her answer could be different. How she'd longed to be in Finn's arms all those years ago. Now, as much as she wanted to dance with him, her legs wouldn't cooperate.

"Don't you want to?"

She noted the insecurity on his face. Finn unsure of himself? "More than you'll ever know," she answered, sorrow evident in her tone.

"Then let's do it." He pushed her chair back and before she knew it, she was upright, and being led to the dance floor.

"Stand on my feet," he said pulling her close, lifting her off the floor.

She did as she was told and suddenly, they were dancing, swaying to the music, fitting together as if they'd been made for one another.

Settling her cheek against his chest, the steady thump of his heart reassuring her, she smiled. "I've always liked dancing." *And I've always wanted to dance with you.*

"I've been waiting a long time for this, and before you give me some cock and bull about just being nice to you, listen to me. When I went to Queen's, I expected to come back, but my parents moved to Ottawa, and every time I made the trip here, you were gone. Once you were at summer camp. Another time you'd gone on that exchange trip to Quebec City for the summer. Then, when I came back after your graduation, you'd left for Toronto. The next thing I knew, your beautiful face was splashed up on billboards all over the country."

"Not so beautiful now," she said bitterly.

He pushed her away slightly to look at her. "What are you talking about? If anything, you're more beautiful than ever. I've dreamed of running my fingers through those golden curls and drowning in your purple eyes for as long as I can remember."

"You've dreamed of me?" It didn't seem possible. Hope filled her.

"You don't get it, do you? I wanted to ask you to the senior prom, but you weren't sixteen yet, and I was afraid your parents would object. Rosie knew how I felt and agreed to speak to your parents. By the time she did, Peter Gwynn had asked you..."

"And you took Mallory Hunter to the prom."

"Bad timing, but for the record, she took me."

"I'd have gone with you if you'd asked," she said softly. "Why didn't you try to find me in Toronto?"

"I did, but I was worried you wouldn't remember me. I was a dumb jock and you were... Each time I got up the nerve up to call, your agent said you were out of town on a shoot or at a premiere. I was all set to try one last time when your engagement made the papers. Lousy timing. I figured I'd missed my chance again. Then I broke my leg and came back here."

Tears shimmered in her eyes. "You should've left a message. I'd have called you. Now, it's too late."

The music stopped, and he looked down at her. "Is it?" *Unchained Melody* played and he started to move again.

The wool of his jacket was smooth beneath her hand. His palm caressed hers while his left hand held her waist. His spicy aftershave was an aphrodisiac, and she wanted him as she'd never wanted anything before. She closed her eyes and let herself savor the moment before answering.

"Isn't it? Look at me. I can't even walk on my own.

Who'd want a girl who may never be able to do anything physical again?'

"I would. I've been searching for her for fifteen years," he said. "She's finally slowed down enough to let me catch up."

Tears slipped down her cheeks. "You're serious, aren't you?"

"I am. I intend to be there for you through thick and thin, and I won't ever let you go. I've loved you half my life, Iris. This is our time now. Give me, give us, a chance."

This felt so good, so right. She nestled into his arms.

"Yesterday's gone, today's almost over, but there was always tomorrow."

"This is tomorrow." He bent his head and claimed her lips.

Spicy Pumpkin Soup

1 tablespoon olive oil
1 red onion, chopped
3 cloves of garlic, crushed
2 large yellow fleshed potatoes, peeled and chopped
2 ½ lbs. of pumpkin, peeled and chopped
¼ tsp. dried red chili flakes
2 tsps. ground coriander
1 quart low sodium chicken stock
½ cup heavy cream
Additional cream and chives to decorate each serving
Toast points or crackers

Directions:
1. Heat oil in a saucepan over medium-high heat. Add onion and garlic. Cook, stirring, for 3 minutes or until onion has softened. Add potato and pumpkin. Cook, stirring occasionally, for 5 minutes or until potato starts to brown. Add chili and coriander. Cook for an additional minute.

2. Add stock. Cover. Bring to the boil. Reducing the heat level, simmer for 10 to 12 minutes or until potato and pumpkin are tender. Set aside to cool slightly. (3-5 minutes)

3. Blend the potato and pumpkin until smooth. Return the pan to low heat and stir in the cream. Heat until warm throughout. Add salt and pepper to taste.

4. Divide into bowls and top each serving with a splash of cream and chives. Serve with toast points or crackers.

Makes 4 servings.

Dinner in the Dark
Rachael Stapleton

Dublin, Ireland
February 14, 2000

"Our dinner plans are confirmed!" Leslie squealed, and hung up the phone.

I shook my head at her. "You really want to do this?" I was unsure why I'd agreed.

"Yes! There are going to be six delicious men—or rather five, plus Paddy."

"Does Paddy not qualify as a delicious man?" He was over six feet tall with large football shoulders and an easy grin. I'd seen Leslie do worse.

"We already hooked up. He's got some good-looking friends or maybe they're his family. I'm not sure—everyone's a bro," she said, deepening her voice to sound macho.

She hopped up on the breakfast barstool. She was five foot nothing and dwarfed by the tall counters of the regency styled home.

"How are you renting this place? It's gorgeous. Last time I checked you hadn't won the lottery."

"Good deal." She nodded, and shoveled a piece of French toast into her mouth.

It never ceased to amaze me how someone so small could eat so much.

"Patrick's uncle owns it and lets him live here for free. I've been throwing him a few bucks once a week. I'm heading out soon—gotta follow that wanderlust where it takes me."

Patrick I assumed was Paddy, one of her three roommates and the one who had invited us to join him for this blind group date that required twelve people.

Technically I was single since my boyfriend and I had just broken up for the millionth time, which was why I'd flown to Ireland to spend Valentine's Day with my best friend, but it still felt like cheating.

I walked to the French doors, and looked out at the other rustic brick houses on Leeson Street; it was dotted with couples pushing strollers and walking large shaggy dogs. I couldn't wait to do that. My great grandmother said I was an old soul. I wanted to get married and have babies, yet when I pictured my boyfriend opposite me at the altar I gagged. What a waste of time he'd turned out to be. Apparently wasting time was my specialty because here I was doing it again. I should be home writing a paper. I was working toward my Masters in library science and in addition to being broke—especially now that my boyfriend wasn't funding my trips—I had three assignments due.

I'd just up and taken off depleting the last of my savings, but in my defense I'd hardly seen Les in the last three months and Europe was amazing. There was so much history in a place this old. I pasted a smile onto my face and pretended to be excited for tonight. Perhaps I'd meet the man of my dreams or at least have an evening full of lascivious fun. Leslie was always telling me to let loose although I suspected that had something to do with the fact that she hated my on-again, off-again, shipping heir boyfriend Nicholas Riley Bexx III.

"So what are you going to wear?" I asked, turning to face her.

"A matching burlesque bra and thong, with lace trim. All red. That's the color of love you know."

"What lace?" I laughed and drained my cup.

Leslie had graduated ahead of me and was now in the midst of her year abroad. She was the most unlikely librarian I'd ever met. She certainly looked the part with her straight brown hair and black semi-rimless cat's-eye glasses. Innocent and studious, but give her a few drinks and you'd find her in the corner making out with some dude.

"I thought we were staying in," I pouted. "I didn't bring anything date worthy. What's the dress code?"

"Rated Adult," She replied and placed our dishes in the sink. "It's a Valentine's dinner, c'mon."

I frowned wondering if I had enough money to hit the mall. "So you're saying jeans and a peasant top won't work?"

"You are not wearing that to dinner," she said, tugging my arm. "I have just the dress."

I eyed her petite frame warily as we climbed the stairs to her room. Her waist was a zero and she carried the rack of a Sports Illustrated model.

"Your dress is not going to fit me."

"It will. I just bought it, a light blue halter."

She pulled it from the closet and much to my surprise, it looked about my size.

"It's gorgeous," I said, running my fingers over the glossy sleek satin. "Why don't you wear it?"

"I would love to but it's too tight in the bust. I even bought it a size larger."

I nodded in sympathy. I'd been shopping with Les enough to know what a challenge it was for her to find anything to fit that curvy little body.

"Honestly it's no big deal—it was on sale and obviously meant to be yours—happy belated birthday!" she said, her voice going up several octaves before she let loose her trademark giggle. "You'll look like a modern day Cinderella."

***

We stepped from the cab and I tugged at the bottom of the dress. It was hopeless; no amount of tugging helped. Leslie was barely five feet and while I wasn't tall, she made me look like a supermodel.

"Stop fidgeting! Satin doesn't stretch," she chided.

"Right. Well, I'm pretty sure Cinderella's fairy godmother didn't put her in a dress that showed off her--" I paused to think of a witty word but apparently the bottom half of the dress wasn't the only thing missing.

"--nether regions," Leslie said smugly.

"Yes. What if I need to bend over?"

"Why would you need to do that?"

"Lots of reason—you bend over to tie shoes, don't you?"

Leslie slapped my derriere as I leaned forward to demonstrate. "Cinderella wore glass slippers, silly, she didn't tie her shoes and neither do you—now chillax—you show off more skin in your bikini then you do in that dress."

I frowned. Obviously Leslie's idea of dress code and mine were conflicting. I required a beach and some water to rationalize two strips of fabric as an outfit.

A wave of nervous excitement washed over me as we stepped inside the grand entrance of the restaurant. There was a group of velvet sofas and an armchair to the left. In between them, a roaring fire blazed from a big marble fireplace.

Two men were sitting on the couch. One of them wasn't half bad looking. My heart fluttered. I hadn't been on a date since I'd met Nick in the south of France years ago and even though this was just a group thing, there would still be eligible bachelors there.

"We're here for the fundraising event. I'm Leslie and this is Sophia. We're part of Paddy's group," Leslie announced sweetly.

"Brilliant. Ye're the last to arrive. Paddy's party was just led in."

I chuckled, thinking of adding pickled peppers to the conversation. I enjoyed being a smartass like that, which is most likely why Leslie and I were the best of friends.

"We've got you all matched up." Our hostess turned her charming smile in my direction. "And you're first. You got the prize."

"What do you mean?" I shifted my stance looking from Leslie back to the hostess. "Matched up?"

"This is a blind date fundraising event," she said, pointing to the corner.

I looked to the large red heart-shaped sign.

Going Blind for Love—The Ultimate Blind Dating Experience
Sponsored by the O'Kelley's of Dublin.
All proceeds benefiting the Fight for Blindness Fund

The hostess smiled sweetly and I looked daggers at Leslie before turning back to her.

"I thought this was a group date?"

Leslie coughed into her hand in true guilty fashion.

The hostess laughed. "I don't know what to tell you. Do ye wanna back out, then? I must say I've seen your man and I wouldn't kick him out of bed for eating crackers."

I looked the girl over. Her legs went on forever and it was hard to miss the fleshy mountains popping out of the cowl neck cutout of the dress she was wearing. What were the chances she had good taste in men.

A shorter dark haired girl walked to the desk and stood beside her.

"Sinead, tell this one here, what you said about the bloke from table three.

"Who do you mean, Cu— "

"Ah! Ye can't say his name, remember?"

"That's right. I can't be repeatin' what I said about him then either, now can I?"

She winked and they both laughed.

My interest was sufficiently peeked but I tried not

to grin.

Leslie chimed in. "I'll take him."

"No, she won't," I said firmly.

"Ye'll like him alright." The hostess gave an enigmatic smile and glanced to her left where a man now stood. "This is your waiter, Theo. Please follow him." She turned her attention to Leslie, "Sinead will show you to your table in just a minute."

I gave Les a wave and Theo ushered me through a doorway to our right and down a long and winding corridor.

"I'm told the restaurant is quite grand. It's owned by one of the richest families in Dublin." Theo said, making idle chatter. "Of course, I myself am blind, like all of the servers here tonight, so I can't be sayin' for sure."

We stopped at a side table topped with baskets. There was a large ornate mirror that ran the length of the wall behind it. "Please choose one," he said.

"Excuse me?" I blurted.

"It's a blindfold, just part of the sensory experience."

I pretended that I hadn't just found that out. I was pretty sure I had no idea what I was in for. I chose a lovely blue band with black lace trim.

"Now, Ms. Marcil, this may come as a surprise but not all blind dates go off without a hitch so we ask that for your own safety ye don't use your real name tonight."

"What?" I swallowed hard. Who in the hell was I being paired up with? I guess handsome didn't guarantee sanity.

"Ye're group organizer has chosen a pseudo name for everyone."

I stared into the full-length mirror and smoothed down the hemline of Leslie's dress. I had to admit it was gorgeous: an open backed pale blue satin halter that complimented my shoulders. The ring at the neck was a thick shiny gold disk so no jewelry was necessary although my great grandmother Gigi had a bracelet that would have looked amazing with it. I ran my hand along the sheer black panty hose. I almost didn't feel like myself at all.

What was this heat and sense of empowerment I suddenly felt tingling in my belly? Maybe a pseudo name meant I could use a pseudo personality. I could be more risqué like Leslie. Nick was always accusing me of flirting—maybe I needed to do it on purpose.

"Is your mask on then?"

"Yes," I answered, quickly securing it over my eyes. He took my hand and led me into the next room.

The room doesn't have windows, I thought, probably candle lit, although the blindfold was really doing its job. I couldn't even make out pinpricks of light and I was trying hard to see. The burst of chatter was distracting and I stopped short, alarmed that I was about to bump into something or someone. I lifted my blindfold to check but the room was pitch black.

"I can't see," I whispered.

"I know." Theo whispered back. "That's the point." He toted me another two feet, carefully guiding me around what I could only assume were other tables with couples.

"No, I mean I really can't see," I whispered, my voice becoming anxious. "Why are the lights off?"

We stopped abruptly. "You peeked. That's against the rules." He clicked his tongue at me.

"I know. I'm sorry. I panicked. Being blind is… oh my God…that was rude," I said, suddenly remembering to whom I was speaking.

"It's all right. I know you're not used to the dark. The blindfolds are only to get you accustomed to the idea. You are going to experience a decadent three-course meal as you've never done before—without your sight. It's a new concept the O'Kelly's have been testing—the last two events were such a success that they're thinking of opening a restaurant in Paris and London.

"Why, though?" I asked before I could get my foot out of my mouth.

"It's meant to heighten your other senses. Or so my Da tells me," a man said cutting in. "It also gives fellas like Theo here a respectable job they love, isn't that right?" His voice had an Irish lilt to it, but it was harsh and raspy, barely above a whisper, different from Theo's, much sexier."

"Bang on." Theo said. "Oh, and your remaining senses will be stimulated to savor the smell and taste—not only that—but the conversation is more intimate and you get a better understanding of what individuals who are blind live with.

"Did they pay you to say that?" the mystery man asked with a chuckle.

"Did it sound rehearsed?"

"Nah. I'd help the lady into her seat but I'm afraid I might step on one of ye in the process."

Theo guided me down onto a bench across from the man's voice and I fixed my dress. Why I didn't know. The room was beyond dark. Not a trace of light anywhere. I kept trying to open my eyes. It made me feel crazy for a minute.

"I'm going to reach out my hand now," the man across the table said.

"All right," I agreed, thinking it was a little early to hold hands.

He grasped it gently and shook it. I nodded at my own stupidity. His hand was large and rough.

"It's nice to meet you," I said, trying to keep the nerves from my voice. All I could smell was his cologne—spicy sandalwood mixed with fabric softener. It was making me heady.

"And you must be Aeval. They've brought us a bottle of the bubbly but I've also gone ahead and ordered a bottle of red wine. Do you drink either?"

"Both. Thank you. I should probably admit I've recently fallen head over heels in love with a shiraz-cabernet. Not many others can hold their own next to it.

"So I haven't a chance then. Bawdy hell! Well I'd better go and leave ye to it."

I laughed, not expecting to like him so instantaneously.

"You've got a sense of humor. I'm glad. People without one don't tend to appreciate my wit."

"If ye do say so yerself."

I laughed again. "Why did you call me Aeval? Is that Irish?"

"Didn't Theo tell ye?"

"I hadn't the chance, the two of you were busy getting' on." Theo's voice boomed from the darkness.

"Holy hell man, ye need to wear a bell, ye put the heart crossway in me and you've been earwiggin' us!"

"Ah, would ya get outta that garden!" Theo responded and the champagne bottle opened with a satisfying pop. "Next thing ye know, ye'll be complaining I shoulda warned ye about that."

Two glasses were poured and one was handed to me.

"To this evening." I whispered.

"*Aye*, may it be everything you dream of. *Go n-ithe an cat thú is go n-ithe an diabhal an cat! Slainte*," he said, and our glasses clinked together. As I took a sip, my heart was beating very fast. His voice was so deep and rugged. I pictured him tall and handsome a cream-colored, shawl-collared cabled sweater. "What does that mean? I asked in an effort to keep the brogue coming.

"Direct translation would be, may the cat eat ye and the devil eat the cat."

Before I could ask what exactly that meant, Theo's voice cut in. "Sorry to interrupt but I should get on with it.

Tonight's theme is Gods and Goddesses. Yer name is Aeval and yer man here is Dubhlainn Ua Artigan."

"Dubhlainn," I said, doing my best not to butcher it.

"In front of you," Theo went on, "ye'll find the sliced pan and butter and the starter is amuse bouche so you can use your hands. At the end of the meal, ye'll be after getttin' a card and if you decide ye like one another, ye may check the box sayin' so and we'll put ye in touch. That way there's no pressure. I'm leavin' now and I'll be back in a few minutes with your black bean soup unless you'd prefer the mystery soup."

"Ohhh… that sounds intriguing. Can you give me hint? I really hate minestrone," I said and smiled and then realized that was useless. I never realized how often I used my smile to charm people.

"Do ye like pickles, then?" Theo asked.

"I do and my mouth is watering now that you've mentioned them.

"Brilliant. I'll bring ye the minestrone then."

"Thank you, Theo." Dubhlainn said laughing. "He's a gas, isn't he?"

"He is." I agreed. "Are all Irish as funny and charming as you and Theo?"

"I doubt the guards are funny if you get thrown in the clinker."

"Well, there goes my after-dinner plans. So Dubhlainn, huh? Did you choose these names?"

"Sure look it. Paddy's a wee bit of cute hoor. He must have remembered the posters on my wall."

"Awe. So you have a crush on this Aeval." I said, patting the table in front of me in the hopes of finding a knife.

"Had. I haven't seen the poster in donkey's years. Take mine. I'll have a go at another."

I finished my slice of bread and reached out for the starter. Something cold and wet fell on my other hand as I picked it up.

"Uh-oh. I spilled."

"Grab another. Don't be shy, lass."

This one made it to my mouth and the mixture of fish and garlic instantly made my taste buds sing. "I love this. Is this smoked salmon?"

"It is. Topped with a slice of cucumber and garlic aioli or so I'm told," he said.

"You got the inside scoop. Cheater," I whispered.

"Sounds like we have that in common. I heard you peekin' earlier."

I blushed. Thankfully he couldn't see.

"So who is this Aeval person? A movie star?"

"A movie star, no. She was a prominent goddess also known as the Lady of Sexuality. She was responsible for makin' the men of the area slaves to their wives' sexual wishes."

I took a deep breath.

"Oh dear, I'm more of a bookworm, you know, glasses and a cozy sweater type of girl."

"In Ireland cozy sweaters are a must. Very sexy especially if that's all ye're wearin'. Sorry it's probably a little early for that kind of talk. I'm afraid I already had a couple pints of the black stuff at the bar with the group."

Theo arrived back at our table and I knew because this time he cleared his throat. It sounded like there were others with him and I mentally pictured them clearing the plates.

"In front of you are the dill pickle soup and the grilled beef tenderloin. Tonight's desert is bittersweet chocolate cake or you can choose the mystery dish."

"I'm good with chocolate." I replied.

"I'll take the mystery dish. I'm feeling adventurous."

I was beginning to feel pretty full when I recognized Theo's scent. I was also beginning to think they were right about this whole enlightened senses thing.

"Would the two of you like to dance now?" he asked.

"Are you serious? Won't we bump into the tables?" I stammered.

"There's a reserved area for it. Only one table dances at a time and I will lead you there," he said as the music changed into a slow melody.

"Shall we?" Dubhlainn sked.

"Okay," I agreed, allowing Theo to help me up. I gripped his elbow.

"Now take one another's hand," he instructed.

I felt a large warm hand slip into mine. When we got to the dance floor, he released my hand and for a minute, I panicked at being alone in the dark. It was silly but it was a strange feeling to never become accustomed to the darkness. Then I felt warm fingers slide onto my bare back. I was thankful for the choice of dress as his touch elicited an unexpected shiver.

He drew me close to him. I could feel his heart beating. I had danced with quite a few men in the last six years, weddings, banquets, balls, Christmas parties. I had been stepped on, and forced to endure stilted conversation, but I had never experienced perfection like this. With this man, there was nothing awkward at all. It felt as if we belonged together.

The song ended and he led me back to our table. I already missed the warmth of his breath on my neck.

Then he came and sat on the same side of the booth as me. "Do ye mind?" he asked.

"Not at all—I wasn't ready to sit alone," I admitted.

"I shouldn't be so forward," he said with his sultry Irish lilt. "But I've never felt such a connection with anyone in my whole life."

"Do you think it's the heightened senses? I'm pretty sure I heard slurping noises coming from the booth next to us. Could be the dill pickle soup's a huge success or maybe everyone's connecting."

He laughed then. He had a deep throaty laugh, genuine. "I heard that too. I think we may need to disinfect the place."

"I think you're right. You said "we"… and how did you know the way back?" I asked in a mock accusatory tone.

He laughed again. "I'll let you in on a secret. I know the owners."

"Oh my God—you're not the owner, are you? And here I was asking why earlier."

"No, I assure you I'm not. I'm studying to be an architect. I specialize in castle design and restoration."

"Really! That's fascinating. Are you just saying that because I told you I'm a bookworm so you assume I love castles?

"Do you?"

"Yes, I suppose I do."

He laughed. "Well now, Theo. Did you hear that? My plan is workin'."

Theo arrived at our table and I heard the clink of more dishes being set down. "Coffee and dessert. Enjoy!"

"Oh Theo. I really loved that soup. Could I possibly get the recipe?"

He paused for a minute and said, "I'll ask the owner."

I picked up my fork and took the first bite. Chocolate melted in my mouth. The second forkful was empty. I was afraid to attempt a sip of my coffee.

"So now, Aeval, you love castles and books. Don't keep me in suspense. Are you a writer?"

"No. Close though. I'm studying to be a librarian. I love reading and helping others fall in love with stories."

"A most honorable profession, to be sure, and what is your favorite story?"

"I couldn't choose just one," I heard myself saying. "If we're talking fiction, there is this time travel series I love but if we're talking stories then I think my favorite would have to the legend of the cursed sapphire. A tale my great grandmother often told."

"That sounds familiar," he said. "Does it have a happy ending?"

"I'll make you a deal," I replied. "I'll tell you about it on our next date if you get me the recipe for that dill pickle soup."

"I like that deal," he whispered in my ear and then kissed me. Gently at first, his lips teasing mine, and then hungrily as he felt me responding to him. I had never known that a kiss could feel like this. I had never known what desire felt like, but I was feeling it now, and as I yielded to his kiss, the thought flooded through my mind that I might have finally found real love.

At last, we broke apart breathlessly. I noticed he was breathing as hard as I was.

"Let's drink a toast to our next date."

"And pickles," I said and laughed.

"Hold your champagne up so I can cheers you."

I did as I was told and the champagne tickled all the way through my body. We'd already gone through the whole bottle of red wine he'd ordered.

I leaned forward to kiss him again but before we could go any further, a loud thump sounded to the left of us and someone screamed.

All we could hear was muffled voices and movement.

"Patrick?" a woman shrieked.

"Please make sure your blindfolds are on. We're turning on the lights and it will be quite bright at first. You'll need to adjust," a man said in a commanding tone.

The lights went on and I was excited at the prospect of seeing my date but even with the blindfold, which I'd forgot I was wearing, I had to cover my eyes to block the piercing glare.

Theo suddenly appeared at our table. "Cullen—come with me. It's yer man. We think he's been poisoned and your Da wants ye."

"Which one?" my date said, knocking the table as he stood. "I'm sorry, Aeval, I'll be right back."

I removed the blindfold just in time to see him exit. He was tall with wavy coppery hair and he was wearing a sweater just as I'd pictured.

"Please, everybody stay seated. Do not drink or eat anything. Your servers will come around one table at a time to explain," a woman's voice called. I kept glancing across at the doorway, wondering when my date was coming back.

Finally, Theo returned instead and offered me his arm. "Your date had to go but your friend, Leslie, is waiting out front." I followed him through the double doors out of the dining room and back down the corridor to the front room.

As I walked out the front door, Nick appeared out of nowhere and swept me into his arms.

"Sophia, I'm so happy I found you. Please say you'll forgive me." He peppered my face with kisses. "I flew all the way here. I couldn't let you spend Valentine's Day alone. I missed you. I can't even remember what we were fighting about."

His kisses felt rough and his body foreign, but to be honest, I couldn't remember why I'd been so mad either.

"C'mon babe, let's go home."

I looked around for Leslie. The street crowd was growing larger by the second as the restaurant emptied out. "Leslie already left in the last taxi," he said as if reading my mind. "My limo's over there. I told Leslie I'd get you home safely. You will come home though, won't you, baby? I need you, and Gigi was worried."

I nodded, feeling tired and now also guilty for not telling my great grandmother I was taking off. The champagne had long set in and the euphoria of my mystery man was fading.

"Why hadn't he come back to at least say good-bye?"

I followed Nick to the black stretch limo, bottling and burying the wave of overwhelming sadness that enveloped me.

***

The next day, I put the mystery man from my mind. I made up with Nick, much to the disapproval of Leslie and flew home with him on his private jet. It occurred to me once a couple of years later that Nick might have been involved, but it never occurred to me that someday I might see my mystery man again. Every now and then, before I fell asleep at night, I would conjure up the feel of his arms, and I would replay that raspy lilt in my head. I prayed so many times to see him again. And it was only the other day when I was unpacking one of my husband's old boxes and found a familiar looking blindfold accompanied by a recipe for dill pickle soup, that I put it all together.

Dill Pickle Soup

Serves: Serves 6-8
Ingredients
- ☐ 5-1/2 cups chicken broth
- ☐ 1-3/4 pounds russet potatoes, peeled and quartered
- ☐ 2 cups chopped carrots (smaller dice)
- ☐ 1 cup chopped dill pickles (smaller dice ~ about 3 large whole dills)
- ☐ 1/2 cup unsalted butter
- ☐ 1 cup all-purpose flour
- ☐ 1 cup sour cream
- ☐ 1/4 cup water
- ☐ 2 cups dill pickle juice*
- ☐ 1-1/2 teaspoons Old Bay seasoning (Available in store or make your own. It's just a combo of celery salt, ground bay leaves, fresh ground black pepper, paprika, dry mustard, nutmeg, cinnamon powder, ground cloves)
- ☐ 1/2 teaspoon table salt
- ☐ 1/2 teaspoon coarsely ground pepper
- ☐ 1/4 teaspoon cayenne pepper

Garnish (optional)
- ☐ sliced dill pickles
- ☐ fresh dill
- ☐ black pepper

Directions
- ☐ In a large pot, combine broth, potatoes, carrots and butter. Bring to a boil and cook until the potatoes are tender. Add pickles and continue to simmer.
- ☐ In a medium bowl, stir together flour, sour cream and water, making a paste. Vigorously whisk sour cream mixture (2 Tablespoons at a time) into soup.
- ☐ Add pickle juice, Old Bay, pepper and cayenne. Cook 5 more minutes and remove from heat. Serve immediately.
- ☐ Taste your soup after adding the pickle juice and final seasonings. Add salt if needed.

The Heart of Stone
Elle Marlow

aggie tried to relax, but the truth was the situation wasn't turning out how she expected. She tucked a strand of loose hair behind her ear as she got herself comfortable in the restaurant booth. Cautiously, she flipped through the classified ads, praying that the next ad would be the lifesaver for her and her daughter.

Nothing. An overwhelming sensation threatened to sting her eyes, but she couldn't give into panic right now. It was her decision to take herself and little Reann to a new town for a new life. A decision she couldn't let overrun her emotions. She flipped to the next page and bit hard down on her lip. No matter what, she was going to keep her spirits up. Surely, somewhere, she'd find decent place for her and her daughter to stay for the night. Maybe tomorrow a job would open up.

Sighing to herself, she couldn't understand it. She'd heard this town was desperate for workers. So far, the only jobs she found available were for mechanics so people could fix their cars and get the hell out. A dot of whip cream sailed over the paper and landed right on top of the ad she was reading.

"Sorry, Mommy," Reann said beyond her view. Maggie curled down the top of the paper in time to witness Reann holding her hand over her little mouth trying not to giggle. Beyond her shoulder, a cowboy held an equally big guilty grin on his face, but he seemed intently interested in a cup of coffee steaming in front of him. Maggie stared at him a little longer than she should have. He was a big man, and had nice clothes and a beautiful smile. Maybe this town wasn't so bad after all. Reann's giggle grabbed back her attention.

"You got a great aim, baby girl, but you promised me you'd eat your breakfast before you ate all the whipped cream off your hot chocolate."

"Everything here *but* the whip cream tastes like crap."

Maggie put the paper down and folded her arms across her chest. Reann's astute assessment of breakfast evoked an audible chuckle from the cowboy this time. It was a deep, warm laugh that pulled her gaze from her daughter once more. Blue eyes sparkling with humor met hers head on. As cute as he was, he wasn't helping matters any. She leaned forward so only Reann could hear her words.

"We don't waste food. We don't talk like truckers, and we don't make a scene in a restaurant. Let me get back to my paper so I can find us a place to sleep and a job."

Reann's brows furrowed. She didn't get the hint to keep their voices low, her next words practically coming out in a shout.

"Why can't we get a real house anyway? I don't like hotels, they stink. I want to live on a farm." Her copper eyes pleaded as she spoke. It was hard to argue with this delightful child. Truth was, Maggie was tired of living like they had been as well. There wasn't anything she could do about it. Until she found a job, hotels would have to do.

"I'm sorry, honey. You know the situation. I'm doing the best I can. This won't last long, I promise. Meanwhile, you need to eat and stop entertaining the other customers."

Reann seemed unconvinced, as she copied her by crossing her own little arms in front of her.

"I wish Daddy were still alive. He wouldn't make me eat this breakfast, and he'd buy us any farm I wanted," She picked up a fork and started poking at a ball of hardened scrambled egg. Her tiny freckled nose curled up with disgust.

Maggie couldn't swallow after that. Her daughter rarely talked about her father, but when she did, she managed to do it in such a way that crashed a world of guilt down around her. She knew Reann suffered miserably, but like her, was a fighter, and almost never allowed her pain to show. There would be no scolding her daughter this time, instead, Maggie sat back, lifted her cup of coffee to her lips, and tried like hell to keep her hands steady. When coffee spilled over and burned her skin, she put down the cup and tried the paper one last time. Maybe there was something in there she missed.

"Ma'am?" She didn't notice that the cowboy had got up from his table and was now standing at her side. Her gaze traveled upward. He was staring down at her, a look of concern on his chiseled face.

She swallowed. Something she figured had died with her late husband awoke within her. The cowboy was quite tall, very fit, but most importantly, there was something about his eyes. They bespoke of kindness. She felt drawn to him as if she was attached by invisible strings. It had been a long time since she'd came close to feeling attraction for anyone. Then the skin on her cheeks warmed with shame. Reann's father had only been gone for a year. It was probably too soon for such thoughts.

"Yes?"

"I don't mean to put my nose in where it don't belong, but I'm heading out toward a horse farm right after I pay my bill. I don't mind if you and your daughter would like to tag along. I'll be up there for a few hours picking up a dozen horses and then I'll be coming right back to town. I happen to know they need help and they have room to spare." He then glanced out the windows, obviously looking at her little car laden down with all their belongings.

"I don't mind taking you up there and showing you the place. I don't think your vehicle will make it until the road thaws."

Maggie blinked a few times, wondering if she'd heard him correctly. It was the first time since her husband's passing that any man offered to help her with anything. His perfectly white teeth and big smile seemed sincere, and his offer was too good to be true, but how could she chance involving her daughter with a stranger and accepting this kind of help? She couldn't do it. She shook her head.

"I'm sorry, I really appreciate the offer, but…"

"Please, Mommy? Even if we can't stay, I've never seen a real horse. I want to go."

The cowboy nodded slightly as his blue-eyed gaze dove into hers. A look of understanding passed between them. Maggie held her breath for a moment. She thought for sure she recognized his interest in her. This wasn't right, it wouldn't be appropriate. How could she refuse him and not appear rude or ungrateful? She hoped her dilemma didn't show on her face. Damn, she was either lonely, crazy, or both. Reann looked up at the cowboy and smiled. It was the first time she'd seen her daughter smile all week. She didn't know what to say.

"I don't mind, but I don't want to step on toes either," he added softly.

Right then the town sheriff walked right up to them and held a hand out for the cowboy.

"Our town sure appreciates the donation you left the Cascade House. Those kids sure will appreciate the Valentine's Day party you provided. They can't wait to dig into all that food and candy you sent."

"Ah, I was glad to do it. If those kids need anything else, you be sure to call the farm."

"Well we did try calling to thank you, but nobody answered the phone," the sheriff said, hooking his thumbs into his belt loops.

"Yeah, sorry about that. I need find myself a

receptionist," he said.

With his words, her daughter spun like a top in the booth and glared at her with an accusatory raised eyebrow. Obviously, the cowboy was a good man and there'd be no reason not to agree to go now. Plus, Maggie had been a receptionist for a travel agency back home. She'd be perfect for the job. Maggie felt the breath she'd been holding escape past her lips. She nodded to her daughter in silent agreement.

When the sheriff walked away, the cowboy pushed his hat back on his head and then offered up a hand. His grip was warm and firm.

"My name is Stone Mitchell, ma'am. I know you won't be wasting your time on my offer, since I'm the one who does the hiring. Our cook also makes hot chocolate that doesn't uh, taste like road apples," he said, giving Reann a wink.

Reann squealed with delight. Maggie's skin immediately warmed. Reann needed a filter sometimes. She couldn't stay embarrassed for long because both Stone and Reann simultaneously broke out in laughter that sounded exactly alike. They already acted like two peas in a pod, and apparently, the decision was made without her.

"Please call me Maggie."

***

The wintery countryside flew past the window of Stone's truck. The several mile long drive wasn't awkward at all, since Stone took the time to act as a tour guide. Reann also kept him busy with questions about horses. He answered every one with patience and good humor.

Her daughter continuously nudged her in the ribs when she heard something she liked. She was being nudged a lot. Reann's change of attitude and her interest in Stone, tugged at Maggie's heart and worried her. What if Stone felt pressured by her daughter to fill some kind of void? Obviously, he had overheard the conversation at the diner that they were widowed and alone. She began to wring her hands together on her lap. Relying on the kindness of strangers wasn't something she was used to doing, and Reann seemed so happy that she couldn't help but fret over her daughter somehow winding up hurt.

When the truck stopped in front of the MM Diamond Ranch, Reann flew over her lap to get out. Stone broke out into a warm chuckle as she ignored the snow and took off for a dead run toward the pasture. Horses, more than Maggie could count, trotted up to the fencing to greet the child by blowing frozen air through their nostrils. Her daughter's sounds of awe could be heard even from inside the truck.

"Don't worry about your little one. She'll be fine." Stone said, reading her thoughts.

"I hope so," she said dropping her gaze to her hands. With just the two of them in the truck, the air seemed to electrify. Why was she allowing her thoughts to stray at a time like this?

"I need a full-time job, Mr. Mitchell," she finally rushed out, forcing herself to keep her focus on what really mattered. He nodded. "Good. I need a full-time receptionist. I uh, am not very good with computers and phones. My time is needed out here. There is so much work and my only help are volunteers from the Cascade House. Those kids, well, they are special to me. I used to be homeless too. So, I know where they are coming from."

She marveled at his honesty and his admission, the way he freely gave his trust, despite the cards life dealt him, squeezed the very air out of her. She could learn a lot from him. Trust wasn't easy for her. But, if there was anything phony or underhanded about Stone Mitchell, she had a hell of a time finding it. She felt much better about Reann being here now. There was just something that needed to be said, and she'd better say it before they got any further.

"I know we've just met, and this might seem like I'm putting the cart before the horse, but I can already tell that my daughter is going to attach herself to you. That seems like an awful lot to take on. I mean, your wife or girl…"

"Don't have one of those. How do you think I was able to afford to donate so much to the Cascade House?" He said, his voice lifting with humor. Maggie had to smile.

"So you won't mind if Reann and I live here while I work? She might be a bit bothersome at times."

Stone lifted his gaze to hers and slightly shook his head.

"Not at all. There are always kids running around this farm. They don't bother me. I'm happy to help them."

"Well, Mr. Mitchell, I guess we have a deal then."

"Please call me Stone."

Again, he reached out for her hand. The feel of his long fingers wrapping around hers created goosebumps all over. There was something secure and exciting about Stone Mitchell. Beyond that, she had to wonder if she was dreaming this whole thing.

"You're a good man, Stone."

"Thank you," he said simply.

Their gazes locked and held. Maggie's mind raced back to her grandma and all the things she used to tell her. One of those things was that there was no such thing as love at first sight. But what about friendship? She hoped Grandma would say it was true for friendship. As much as she was attracted to Stone, she needed a friend more. Looking at him, she knew she had one. She also knew that she could have more when she was ready. The realization sent her heart racing a little faster.

They got out of the truck and walked toward the pasture. Stone removed his jacket and laid it over her shoulders. Engulfed in his warmth and the scent of a woodsy cologne, Maggie's head spun slightly. Her grandma also said, life can spin on a dime. Now she believed it.

Reann raced up to them, kicking up a powder of snow, out of breath, and with her cheeks pink from the crisp air. She was smiling and darting her gaze back and forth between the two of them.

"I want to go to the Valentine's Day party the sheriff talked about. I should get to go. I was homeless too—just five minutes ago!"

Stone reached out and playfully roughed up the top of her head. Reann giggled then ran back to the fencing.

Maggie bit down on the inside of her cheek. Stone had turned to face her. When he spoke, it was soft and fluid. He lifted his hand to swipe a stray hair out of her eyes just as it began to snow.

"What do you say Maggie? Will you and Reann be my date for the Valentine's Day party?"

"Absolutely."

Stone's Hot Chocolate

1 cup whole (or 2%) milk
1/2 cup heavy whipping cream
1 1/2 cups cocoa powder
1 tablespoon granulated sugar
1 1/2 teaspoons dark chocolate, grated
1 1/2 teaspoons milk chocolate, grated
1 (14 oz) can sweetened condensed milk
1/8 teaspoon vanilla extract
Whipped cream
Big fluffy Marshmallows slightly toasted over a fire.

Directions:

Pour milk and heavy cream into a saucepan. Heat over medium-high heat. Do not allow to boil.

In a large bowl, mix: cocoa, sugar and both chocolates. Whisk together. Add this dry mix to the milk/cream mixture in saucepan. Whisk to combine. Reduce heat to medium.

Pour in sweetened condensed milk and vanilla. Stir well. Reduce heat to low and simmer for 5 minutes.

Top with a large roasted marshmallow.

Best on a snowy day looking out over a field of horses.

LOVE, FOOD, AND HEAVEN
Vanayssa Somers

*I*t was all a long time ago, she thought, settled in her armchair, the flames in the fireplace popping and sparking comfortably before her. She stretched out her legs, rested her feet on the ottoman, gazed into the flames.

For some reason, tonight she was thinking about him. She hardly ever thought about him anymore. Rob, with his deep brown eyes, hair falling roguishly across his forehead. His smile.

What a womanizer he'd been. And she, so naïve, fresh from the country, thirty-eight years old and hardly even been kissed.

She'd left her parents' home for the first time, when her sister and brother-in-law had decided to give her a break so she could attend the Music Conservatory. Finally. Someone had had to care for the old folk, and as the youngest female, it had naturally fallen to her to fill the job. She'd always liked nurturing, it had come naturally to her.

But they all knew she'd yearned to complete her music education, study fine arts somewhere, carve out her own place in the real world. And so, Evelyn and Harold had come riding to the rescue, letting her spread her wings, such as they were. A loving gift. Typical of her family, close and caring.

But what had she known about the real world? Only whatever she'd learned from books, and you couldn't rely on that second hand knowledge, as she'd learned early on in her worldly explorations.

What really happened was, in her late thirties, she had discovered romance.

On this improbable planet, spinning obscurely through time and space around one of a trillion sun-stars, she'd found a man who loved making love to women. Who loved women, couldn't get enough of them.

She laughed a little, wiggling her warm toes in front of the curling orange flames.

She remembered. Oh yes, she remembered everything.

He'd taught her what it was all about.

Time, space, event. The earth moves, providing all three. After that, it's up to us. We must overcome inertia. Deal with resistance to beginnings and the dull stillness of endings. She'd written:

> *Sitting alone in a grey restaurant*
> *I think about this short tablecloth*
> *Unlike the longest tablecloth in town*
> *Under the shelter of which his cheeky toes*
> *Crept up my thigh, making it hard*
> *To eat clams nicely.*

She'd written a book of poems, unable to remove the living, breathing reality of memory from her heart and mind.

This rare find, this lover of women, was somewhat short and lightly muscular, his skin varnished to antique glow by the suns of Portuguese beaches and Mayan ruins; he wore soft cotton shirts in blistering white or masculine pastels, freshly laundered. He smelled of soap. His skin was velvet, his hair iron-grey. His sheets were printed with bright parrots, and his home reverberated with thick blues and rich saxophones.

He'd stirred the occult kundulini, coiled for decades deep at the base of her spine.

He'd taught her to drink strong, sensual coffee, to shop for good wine at low prices, and to grow basil for homemade pesto, thick with freshest parmesan and garlic. Heavy with the oil of sun-drenched olives.

There was a small restaurant. Set back off the street, modest in appearance. She recognized it from the first; it was the intimate world of daydreams, where picoseconds last forever. A virtual reality place, an escape from stuffy classrooms and family situations, a place you never tell your mother about, she thought, enjoying the heat of the flames, the warmth of her cat on her lap.

And of course, your mother never tells you about those things either, but you both know; the daydream blueprints which suffuse everyone's youths with rosy forward-looking.

To make those dreams come true requires another presence, an opposite energy, fully accepting, magicked by your being there. Time, place, and persons; the explosive compounds of experience, spinning memory-galaxies, the knitting of infinite effect.

In their cafe were aromatic herbs, crusty hot breads, immense bouquets of dried flowers, green silk willow trees, melding their energy fields into a potage of beguilement.

With Capricorn appetite, she had spooned greedy gobs of garlic mayonnaise. Clam and mussel shells, gleaming wetly, littered wide bowls of thick, tomato-ey bouillabaisse. Lights gleamed ruby-red through wine glasses against heavy white tablecloth, munificent lengths of fabric draping her toes.

The tender meat of clams and fantasy, and brown, brown eyes. All of it now irrevocably drifted off, like rain-forest mist, into what we call the past, when Earth had danced her sun-moon two-step only a thousand million times. When the Sun was younger.

His eyes, deep brown, were both deep and soaked with brownishness. Immersed in thought. How to approach that night's exacting of mutual satisfaction. Gazing imperturbably at her through pipe smoke from the far end of his oaken kitchen table.

"Turn away thine eyes from me, for they have

overcome me…"

Romantic love, say historians, was invented in the West, along with the Model-T Ford's mobile privacy. They overlook the Bible's love-song of Solomon. And Sarah was well versed in the Bible. Oh yes, she had had a blessed upbringing. Loving parents, godly home.

She knew all about Solomon. Another man who loved women, really loved them. *Loved us*, she thought, a small smile slipping around her lips.

The cat stretched luxuriously in the heat of the flames, sighed deeply and curled up in a new position on her lap.

Whatever else he was writing about, the scent of Woman-Lover drifted from those rice-paper biblical pages. She scratched kitty's neck, tickled his ears. Sighed. She'd read her share of Cosmo and other glossy, sensual magazines. No richly scented modern day magazine, screeching new routes to female orgasm, had ever equaled that ancient Biblical libido-stirring incense.

Between the night her lover's brown eyes locked with hers over the bouillabaisse, and this particular still winter night, stood twenty-three years of earth time.

Time had "passed" as they say, since the events in that short poem…almost 8,400 days. Or, 3,626,608 seconds. More or less.

Every single American bear had hibernated, in secret caves she would never know about, twenty-three times. A lot of Zees.

In far Alaskan wastes, birds, whales, sea lions and enemy warships had gone about their destined affairs time and again. The man-faced moon had cast its womanly length along iceberg littered seas in obedience to her kitchen calendar an exact number of times.

Millions, whatever that meant, of children in Rwanda, Darfur, Somalia and the Balkans, had spent the twenty-three years in intensive time-management training.

Carrying guns, running for cover, burying family, searching for love. What a schedule, she thought, briefly comparing her own protected, guided childhood to theirs. She shook her head. Some things. No one would ever understand.

In purdah, Islamic women the world over had dreamt their own two-hundred and seventy-six months' worth of dreams. She suspected their reveries differed in tense—passive, as opposed to her own active. Not finding, but being found by, a man who loves women.

My prince will come, the universal song.

What is this persistent thing, this profound calling to Romantic Love, to the possibility of starting each day awash in worship of another? We dream on, wanting it to be so, trying again and again.

Her Biblical training in church and home had lent her considerable wisdom and breadth of thought concerning the path of profound romantic human love. Worship. We crave it as we crave chocolate, fresh warm bread, melted butter, homemade jam.

Of course. We were created with that large G-spot deep in our psyche and our soul. The need to look up to, to find someone worthy of our soul, of our immortal beingness. To breathe in a new rhythm, in rhythm synced to another's breath, sacred breath.

The breath of the beloved. Above, in sacred, inaccessible vaults, in an unknown, unknowable place, the place we were truly conceived to begin with.

As above, so below.

And so we seek another breath to match our own to, the march of another's chest rising and falling through the seconds and minutes of our life-shift on the blue planet, spinning, spinning, breathing.

However, to succeed in this search for such a beloved, we must be more flexible than we know how to be, and we must become open to change. And change she had.

He had re-formed her, body and soul, for the two-year expanse of time she'd spent in his tutorial company. And how she had learned. Learned, yes, her country girl mind lit like volcano-flame as each new milestone in passion and giving, taking, giving, taking, breathing, breathing together.

She'd loved his hands so much. Strong, gentle, precise, knowing, experienced. Oh yes, very experienced. She laughed a little, stretched out now by herself, just she and her kitty, her comfortable, cozy home around her, warm and safe in her ageing years.

Warm and safe. But how she'd loved that stretch into danger. Into the red, heated, heart of romantic love. Her first experience.

And there'd been others. But never again, anyone like him. He was the first, it was true, and the first is forever etched on our memory banks.

But more than just the first. In his profession, powerful. In his friendships, exotic people, people she would never have normally met. In his travels, sophisticated, gourmet, wide-ranging.

Physically, a specimen. Golden, fit as any racehorse, smallish. Not that tall, she mused, remembering how he fit her, stretched out on the multi-colored bedding, his length about the same as hers, just maybe a little taller than she herself.

His mind was the author of his power. Intellect, dazzling. Wit, intimidating. Kindness, overarching.

Oh, she had learned about love. She had loved him in that mesmerized way only an innocent country girl can love in the presence of a truly large human being.

But, time goes on.

As her own form and function changed in response, she saw her journey inside the ultimate love affair with new eyes, expanded vision, more comprehensive desires.

She had begun to want her own power. Her own

pathway. Just being with him so much opened within her psyche a burning need to find out how far she could go, what wonderful things she herself might create.

She had done what adults so often do in a deep, life changing relationship... she had outgrown her lover, her idol, her idyll.

She had left him behind.

Oh, not in literature, not in anything related to his own profession or expertise.

No, she had become more than that; she had become her own woman. Someone who would have been a total stranger to the girl she'd been when they first met.

And, in the Conservatory, unknown territory to him, she had excelled and glowed, taken a Mentor, a new Teacher.

A teacher who took her deeper, not into himself, but into herself. A teacher uninterested in romance, but passionate about music, about composing, about perfection.

And so her lover had experienced desperate jealousy and outrage; she had seen, at last, the weakness in him. He had never thought it possible... there was a force in life, a power, somewhere, that he could not compete against.

He could not win.

In the end, she had gently and with regret, but deep assurance, kissed him goodbye one last time, her lashes soaked with tears, her face wet.

It wasn't just sex. Oh no. Sex that consumed while it grew whole fields of wildflowers in her being, wafted perfumes into her soul she had hitherto never dreamed of.

Romantic love that had opened her knowledge to an expanse of feeling, of emotion, of human-ness she hadn't known existed.

How does one thank someone for such a gift?

How would the country girl of Solomon's Song have thanked her King for the indelible transformation in her existence?

After the Song was over.

After the last trembling verse of devotion, of passion, had drifted out into space, like mist that no heat could vanish, ever.

Oh yes, she still could bring back the feelings. The music. The taste of his red wine. The scent of the roses he first gave her in a long box, the first lover's bouquet she had ever been given, that little country girl.

And she could twist the blazing blue sapphire ring on her third finger, left hand, watching the firelight flicker in its considerable depths. A rare jewel, he had called her more than once, gazing into her eyes across the table in their French restaurant. Their favorite place.

Where he would slip his shoe off and use his toes, under the snowy lengths of linen tablecloth, to tease up her thigh, lifting the hem of her blue dress, the one he liked the most. Flaring round her hips when they danced, floating as they walked quiet streets at midnight together, the way the silky fabric brushed across her bare bottom as she moved with him from the candle-lit table to his bedroom.

Oh, he had taught her well. About so many things.

But most of all, he had taught her how large a being she herself was; what depths, what expanses, lay within her own mind and heart.

He had taught her to go where he himself could never go, into the far spacious reaches of all that music could offer, and beyond.

Music.

Now, that was love.

She smiled again, stroking kitty, who, annoyed at the gentle intrusion, stretched again, got up, and jumped off her lap.

She sighed. It was good to remember. She would always remember.

It was good to enter her ageing years with many,

many fine memories. Her sixties were not far off now.

Much like having a wine cellar full of the best the world's vineyards had to offer.

Her turn to stretch.

She got up, put the screen in front of the fireplace carefully.

One had to be careful with fire.

It could burn the house down if left untended and unguarded.

She had never let that happen.

No, her house was in fine shape.

And her memories also.

She stood absently at the bottom of the staircase, gazed up at the shadows above. Where her exquisite bedroom awaited her nightly routines.

There was no one waiting for her in that room, with its silks and velvet fittings, its view of the ocean, its fine furniture, its crystal chandelier.

For a moment, her head dipped, sadness outlining the lines of her face briefly. It was all in the past now.

But, as always, she thought of the morrow ahead. The sun rising once more, as he had always said. A new day ahead, little girl, he would say, stroking her hair lovingly. It's always new. Never believe anything else.

There's always something new ahead, even on our final day.

New music to hear, new lines to compose.

And one day, she would stand in some far distant, vaulted place, alight with the light of a thousand suns. Surrounded by joy she could not, at this moment, comprehend.

And all he had taught her of love, love in all its many forms and purposes, would stand her in good stead on that day.

For, she felt sure, her own light would shine as bright as any sunrise ever could.

And without him, she would never have shone so bright, so far.

So she stood at the base of the stairs, moving her left hand, watching light move in the engagement ring he had allowed her to keep when she had finally walked away.

Walked away, ready for a sunrise she alone could experience, and only by herself.

But she had turned her head, walking away that day.

Turned fully, stood, looking back. She hadn't turned into a pillar of salt, no.

He stood, watching her as she'd walked away. Knowing. Smiling, knowing he was watching a creation of his own, moving into a new kind of world.

With his blessing.

Well, of course. She sighed.

There had always been the others. The other women.

He just loved women.

She smiled as she began to climb the stairs. Yes, he certainly had.

Filled with the warmth of remembered love, Sarah slipped between her expensive sheets, turned to watch a full moon over the ocean.

Wherever he was tonight, if still on earth after all these years, he watched the same moon.

If he'd gone on before her, he would be young again, virile and beautiful, just like he used to be.

Perhaps, even, who knew...

Waiting for her?

PESTO

First of all, you will need to buy a mortar and pestle if you don't have one already. Ideally, that is.

Before you, spread out on your kitchen counter, will be the ingredients:

Basil, which you will have grown in a pot on your window sill. Again, ideally.

As many cloves of garlic as you think you will enjoy.

Pine nuts. Some prefer almonds, but pine nuts make it creamier.

Salt, of course.

Fresh parmesan cheese you will have bought from an Italian deli, fresh.

Olive oil, the kind of your choice.

Now you pound together with your mortar and pestle the garlic and pine nuts.

Then, add the basil leaves, as many as you want, and salt.

Pound the mixture again till creamy.

Finally, the parmesan cheese, and you will need olive oil to help meld the parmesan nicely into the mix.

That's it.

Great on any kind of pasta, also on bruschetta. Even on toast if you like strong flavor.

Chains of Magic
Margaret Egrot

(With thanks to William Shakespeare for the characters and help with the script)

Senator Brabantio felt he should send his daughter to her private chambers when he realized that Othello, a man of color, would be among his important guests that night. He wasn't sure what worried him most. Was it only Africans he needed to worry about—or Asians too—or maybe Muslims of any color—or all of them? All his instincts and upbringing told him he must protect his daughter. Aside from any germs they might carry—or outbreaks of unprovoked violence—there was their attitude to young girls and women. And, oh yes, their gross clasps, their foul charms, their drugs…

His dear wife would have known how to tell the difference between the civilized guests and the drug dealers or rapacious ones, but she had died years ago, leaving him to bring up their only daughter and find her a suitable husband on his own. He was sure his wife would never have regarded a man of color as a suitable potential husband, but would she have permitted a certain amount of social contact? He puckered his lips anxiously and wished for the millionth time that she were still here to tell him what to do.

Brabantio loved his daughter dearly. He had watched proudly, if timidly, as she grew from a sweet and docile little girl, into an attractive, if sometimes argumentative, adolescent. Now she had blossomed into a beautiful and charming young woman who sat next to him at table as the lady of the house on those occasions when he was required to entertain visiting dignitaries. She was proving to be a great success in this role too: excellent at organizing the meals and servants so that it all ran smoothly, modest and discrete with all the gentlemen guests, caring and considerate for their wives—knowing just when it was time to leave the men to their port and affairs of state. Her presence at these functions had taken a great weight from his shoulders, and he couldn't imagine now how he would manage without her if she ever did marry and leave him to run someone else's household.

But he had other things to worry about tonight. This Othello, the celebrated Moor of Venice, the brave general, was due to visit. True, he was not a young man—almost the same age as Brabantio himself. And he was definitely a very important person. But he was black. Very black. A Muslim, too, by all accounts. Should he run the risk? Would he not still, despite his age and rank, exude some kind of dusky charm that would intoxicate a young woman? Even one as shyly modest and level headed as Desdemona? He wrung his hands. No, he couldn't take the risk.

Then what? How would he get through the evening on his own? Wouldn't all his usual guests notice her absence and find it strange? How would he explain why she wasn't there? Would they laugh and think him old fashioned if he gave his reasons? What sort of embarrassment to the state would that cause, if the great Othello himself found out?

But what if she did attend? Wouldn't those same guests accuse him of being careless with her reputation in letting her sit at table with such an exotic? Would she be tainted by such contact? Would that make her less easy to marry to someone suitable? If only that young man who was so intent on wooing her at the moment wasn't such a drunken fop. If only Desdemona had shown some sign she was remotely interested in his attention. Why, then he could have agreed the match months ago and wouldn't have all this worry. True, he had told this—what was his name? Roderigo?—himself that he didn't want him as a son-in-law. Despite the young man's rank and background, he was not the upright and intelligent man he had envisaged as suitable for his daughter. But he wouldn't be in this quandary if Desdemona was now betrothed to him, or someone like him. Perhaps he should have tried harder to encourage the courtship. Oh, if only his dear wife were here… Or if only the lusty moor (for he was sure he must be that, despite his age) could be sent off quickly on some new campaign so wouldn't have time to dine with him tonight. He wrung his hands again and groaned.

"What is it, Father?" Desdemona had entered without him hearing. She kissed him gently on the cheek. "Still worrying about affairs of state? I'm sorry I can't help you there, but I have sorted the seating plan for dinner tonight." Brabantio jumped as if shot. "Oh, my dear daughter, I'm not sure you should be there at all. What would your dear mother…"

"I'm sure Mother would have been at your side, as I will be." Desdemona replied firmly. "Why, do you think the noble Othello is going to try and cast a spell on me over the soup?" She laughed merrily, and Brabantio joined in weakly.

"It's true, I'm dying to meet him, to hear from him about his adventures—Has he really met people who carry their heads beneath their shoulders? And he is so brave by all accounts."

"He is a noble man, as good as any." Brabantio agreed hesitantly. "But, daughter, he is black. Such men aren't like the rest of us; they cast spells on young women… minerals… medicines…"

"Which is why I have placed him next to me, in case any of our female guests are nervous, or he lacks those soft parts of conversation they are used to."

"Oh, daughter!" Brabantio looked aghast, and Desdemona patted him affectionately.

"Dear father, don't be so old fashioned! I'm a grown woman. And, apart from anything else, he is so old! No, you just leave the arrangements for the evening to me. I'll see that he is properly entertained according to his rank and fame. I'll get cook to serve your favorite pudding— grilled figs with butter and honey and a sprinkle of cinnamon, just how you like them. Now I'm sure you have plenty of other things to do today. You just go and sort your state papers out for the next senate meeting. And don't worry!"

She ushered him gently toward his office, pecking him on the cheek again before dropping a brief curtsey and departing towards the kitchen to have a word with the housekeeper and head cook.

Brabantio hesitated before entering his office. He had felt helpless to argue. Desdemona could be very persuasive when she wanted to be and, in truth, he really loved sticky fig pudding. He would have been lost without her to sort the dinner arrangements. But was it what his wife would have agreed to? Would she herself have sat down with a black man, however noble? And would she have allowed her unmarried daughter to sit next to one? He doubted it. Oh dear, what troubles had he unleashed upon himself? He was sure no good was going to come of such a break from custom. His daughter would be doomed to spinsterhood, and he would be the laughing stock of Venice.

Sighing and wringing his hands even more desperately than before, he finally entered his office and spent the rest of the day wrestling with his nervous indigestion, blinking queasily at his papers, deferring any important decision till he felt better, and praying to God and any saint who might be listening, that the evening would pass without incident. If only his dear wife was still around to tell him what to do…

***

Desdemona meanwhile spent a productive afternoon discussing menus with the cook, supervising the preparation of the dining hall, and arranging table decorations with her lady in waiting. She was excited. Most of the dinners her father held were dull affairs with elderly men and their elderly wives in predominance. The talk was always about politics and commerce, in neither of which she had any interest. Sometimes she struggled to stay awake and the talk, when the ladies withdrew and wanted to discuss the servant problem or their ailments, was scarcely more enlivening. But tonight there would be the great Othello himself and other serving soldiers of rank— the conversation was bound to be more thrilling, both during and after the meal.

She wouldn't dare to say anything herself of course. She was still shy and blushed profusely when directly addressed, which made her even more tongue-tied. There was so much she would like to ask the general, and she hoped her father and his friends would be as curious as she was to know more of his adventures and the places he had visited. Maybe she could prompt her father before the meal. Or would he think her too interested, too immodest even, and all his worries about her being there at all would resurface? No, perhaps she had better leave it to fate. After all, if Othello was to be in Venice for any length of time, he would have to be invited again. It might take time for her curiosity to be satisfied, but she was patient, and a good listener.

She was a good organizer too. She was quite confident in her ability to ensure all the guests were well looked after. The cook had told her the general probably wouldn't eat pork or shellfish so she had opted for roast swan, lamb, and venison with a wide range of baked, boiled and steamed vegetables. All washed down with the best wine her father's cellar could offer. Plenty of choice would ensure there would be something to suit everyone's taste.

The main courses would be followed by the sponge and sorbet gateau, decorated in true Venetian style, the cook had promised for dessert. To finish, there would be plenty of fruit: dates from North Africa, grapes and oranges from Spain, even a few apples from England, though they were now a little soft following their long journey. And, of course, the grilled figs.

She heard her stomach rumble as she thought of the feast to come. She had been too busy to stop for lunch, and now she needed to go and bathe and dress for the evening. There would be no harm, surely, in her wearing her new gown, and her mother's lovely pearls that her father had given her when she came of age? She was not particularly vain and rarely took long over her toilet, even for important functions, but she knew the pearls showed off her long, delicate, white neck to advantage, and the rich azure brocade of her dress matched exactly her blue eyes. She had a premonition that it was going to be a night to remember, and she wanted to dress the part.

**

Although she had confidently assured her father that it was best to place Othello next to her so as not to offend or upset any of the other female guests, Desdemona found herself even shyer than usual at table, and far too nervous to look directly at their special guest. But she soon realized that, although he had spoken to her civilly on arrival and she had murmured a few words in response, there was no need for her to speak at all. The questions from the men were all about Othello's exploits and he was happy to elaborate on them. She listened, gripped, as he told them of his battles, sieges, and accidents. His capture and escape from slavery, his travels and his meetings with cannibals—and yes, he really had been to the land where there were men whose heads grew beneath their shoulders. Desdemona was so engrossed she could hardly breathe. She often forgot to signal to the servants to clear the plates for the next course and had to be prompted by the chief steward. Her father had to remind her twice that it was time for her to retire with the other ladies.

Only as she rose to leave the dining hall did she pluck up enough courage to look directly at Othello and, with a small sigh, express her sorrow for the sufferings he had endured and admiration for the courage he had shown in combating them. He had risen too, bowing to her as she left the table and taking her hand to kiss. She did not resist and as she caught his eye, he smiled at her with such attentiveness that her heart raced and she felt the blood rushing to her cheeks. Not just a man of courage, she knew instinctively he must also have a constant, loving, and noble nature. No one could look at a woman like that if they did not. He was just the kind of brave but tender man she had dreamt of for a husband. She blushed more deeply than she had ever done before, confused, and embarrassed by this unbidden train of thought. Quickly she withdrew her hand from his and almost ran out of the room without looking back. The other ladies hurried after her.

***

The men seemed to take forever over their port and conversation dragged amongst the ladies. They too had all seemed fascinated at table by Othello's tales, but were too refined to be the first to mention him or them. Yet other topics seemed pallid by comparison. Desdemona tried to show an interest in her companions' health and family doings, but her mind was elsewhere and she was relieved when, finally, her father called to say the men were ready to go. She rallied a little then to bid her guests farewell and wish them safe journeys home, but retreated to her chamber as soon as the last one had departed. Normally she and her father would chat a little together each night before retiring but it was late and, she reasoned, he would be tired—his health was not good and the dinner would have been a strain for him.

Desdemona herself was not tired. She was glad her lady in waiting had been in already to turn down the covers and light the small bedside lamp. She changed quickly into her nightdress and climbed into bed. She had no desire to read, but instead closed her eyes and thought back excitedly over the conversation at dinner. Othello had lived a life so different from her own and her father's. Neither of them had been beyond the city walls in her lifetime as Brabantio had been reluctant to travel on business and he was now far too old to be called up for combat.

The stories Othello told of strange lands and extraordinary incidents had been a feast in themselves, but she was hungry for more. Such dangers had he faced and lived to tell the tale! Her father must invite him again—and again. She was sure he would, but if he were reluctant, she would use all her subtle powers to persuade him. Of course, she realized, to seem too interested would only worry Brabantio, so she would have to be careful.

Othello's stories had cast a spell on her but she was going to learn from this and use her own charms on her father to ensure the noble general was invited again. She would remind her father that the moor was destined to be of continuing service to the state so he, Brabantio, leading senator, was obliged to entertain him generously. She could organize bigger and better meals on his behalf, and could hide her curiosity behind her customary maidenly modesty whilst finding out more about the man she loved.

She gasped and sat up straight in bed. Love! What was she thinking! Othello, The Moor of Venice, could have no thought of marrying her, a mere slip of a girl - and white as a lily too. Besides, she had been too shy to speak to him that evening, and would never be allowed to be alone in his company nor did she know anyone she could confide in, or use as a go-between.

How could he get to know of her passion without her courting criticism for forward behavior? Maybe he would know anyway, without her needing to say anything, and would ask one of the young officers who accompanied him to dinner to intercede? Her father would see nothing amiss there. After all, he was not averse to her finding a husband. She thought of all the other young men, potential noble matches, that he had suggested - and whom she had dismissed as too boring.

As for her latest suitor... Her nose wrinkled in disgust. She was glad her father did not like him either, and had told him his daughter was not for him. But it was someone of his ilk, if somewhat more sensible, that her father would definitely want her to settle down with eventually. Some one of rank and standing in the city: steady, industrious, ambitious, careful. He would happily marry her to such a man, and stand by proudly as she set up her own household and produced several grandchildren for him over the years. It was a life she had envisioned for herself with equanimity, if not actual enthusiasm. Until now. Now she would rather die than end up with such a fate. It was the moor or a convent for her. No other man would do.

Dare she forsake her friends and father? Surely they would not approve of such a match. Dear father, the shock would kill him! Her confidence failed for a moment—she really loved her father and did not want to hurt him—but he would never consent to such a son in law, and it would be dangerous to her cause to ask him to consider it. However, his anxieties and hesitancy about all the little things in life would drive her mad if she had to live at home much longer. Were already driving her crazy, she had to admit. She yearned to be at the side of a man of action, a man of passion – her lusty moor! She stifled a giggle—what was she thinking of?

She would have to use her own chains of magic to draw him to her, until he and he alone could see her love for him, and reciprocate. They would have to elope of course, and then cast their fate upon the mercy of the senate. But it would be worth it. She would marry the moor, or die in the attempt.

By now she was quite tired, and the excitement of the early evening was catching up with her. Yawning, she drew her white silk sheets up around her chin with one hand and smoothed them down over her breasts and thighs with the other. Just like a wedding dress, she thought dreamily as she looked down on her white-draped shapely body. Soon, she thought, I will be fast asleep. Dear God, will it be a sin if I dream of such a secret courtship, of strange lands, and of this man who now seemed to her to be more fair than black?

Othello would be coming to the house again very soon, she was sure of it; the next day even. Tomorrow! Yes, tomorrow was when she would start her campaign to charm him into loving her. She would ask cook to prepare something special. Not oysters of course, as Othello would not be able to eat the shellfish, however delicious, but something just as powerful. Asparagus perhaps? Her newly betrothed friend had sworn by them. Asparagus tips steamed until just al dente to retain their potency, then lightly tossed in melted butter and sprinkled with flower pollen.

And if that didn't work she would cast her own spells and win him with magic. She could! She should! She would! He was the breath of life to her. Smiling happily to herself, she reached up and put out the light.

Recipe for Grilled Sticky Cinnamon Figs

Ingredients

8 ripe figs
Large knob of butter
4 tablespoons of clear honey
1teaspoon of ground cinnamon

Method:
Heat the grill to medium heat.
Cut a deep cross in each fig and split apart (like a flower)
Place the figs in a baking dish and drop a small knob of butter on each fruit.
Drizzle honey over each.
Sprinkle a dash of cinnamon over each.
Grill for 5 minutes until the figs are softened and the honey and butter make a sticky sauce in the bottom of the dish.
Serve warm with a scoop of ice cream, whipped cream, plain yogurt, or crème fraiche.

The Moon and The Daystar
Cynthia Ley

I was in college, senior year. Everything, to me, was anticipatory. I was on the edge of freedom, unsure of my road. I knew I wanted more than the 1950's American dream. That world still influenced us, more than sixty years after the fact. I guess that if I had been a college kid back then, I would have been part of the Beat Generation, hanging out in basement coffee shops, drinking bad espresso, listening to poetry and chain smoking. I did not want a traditional life.

So what did I want? Toward what future was I gravitating? These are things I pondered in my local coffee shop each morning before heading off to class. I meditated on the frothy foam atop my latte and envied it its lightness, the ease with which layers broke through to each other and combined with grace. What was holding me back?

I needed a kindred soul. And just like that, one emerged.

One morning, I rose very early, unable to sleep. Very little stirred in the pre-dawn hours of a cold winter day. I bundled up and went to school with my accustomed coffee drink in hand, having picked it up along the way. My first class wasn't due to start for another hour, so I sat on a bench out on the athletic field, looked up, and watched the darkness seek out the light.

"I love coming here too," a warm voice murmured.

I turned to her, startled but not frightened, and looked into a pretty face in all its natural candor, full of life and eagerness. Her warm brown eyes sparkled, and her rosy cheeks were precursors to the coming dawn. She too held her coffee in both hands, warming them.

"I'm Stella, Stell for short," she offered, smiling. "I'm in your trig class."

I always sat at the back of the room; all I ever saw were heads in front of me. "I'm Aurelia, Aurie for short," I said. "Blackboard jockey?" referring to the kids who sat in the front row.

"Yeah," she laughed, then teased, "Door jockey?"

I grinned. "Yeah. Hate math."

"Me too."

We settled back on the bench and watched the day unfold.

***

That was the first time I'd ever felt a really deep connection with someone my own age. We made a standing date to meet early at the coffee shop every morning, and go to our bench and immerse ourselves in the world as the weather permitted. We watched Nature reveal herself in all her honesty.

Stell wanted to be an artist—she showed me her portfolios and she was very good. My love was writing. With pencils and paper, we sketched each experience, walking inside the sunbeams, being transformed by the fog. It all made sense to us, this marvelous taking in of life in the everlasting now.

And after, we talked. Our coffee shop was our home base, our place to share our unique expression with each other. We would sip the rich brew and look into the face of the other, conjuring the images of those moments, which sparked us to life. I told her stories from her pictures; stories, she said, that were in her mind as she drew. "We are spinners, you and I," she said.

"We share a brain," I laughed. For it was true. It didn't matter that we created in different mediums, or that we were each our own artist. Stell's world was one of color and form, mine of sound and image. They courted each other in new dances during those brief and exquisite moments when they shared the same celestial space. Fleeting though their contact might be, our arts touched and our souls fell in love. Over and over and over.

And our bodies? I don't think either of us thought about the other that way. We were two young women who knew that love and lust were two different creatures. As for us, we were twins, speaking our own language. We didn't care if anyone else understood it. It wasn't meant for them. Each was the axis of the other. So we spun—sometimes fast, sometimes slow, but always in sync.

Over time, we began to collect an audience. From the very beginning, we had recorded our sessions so as not to lose any part of our collaborations. The shop owners didn't mind—they said we were good for business, and asked if we could keep a schedule so others would know when to find us there. College students, at first. Then some of our teachers came, and it wasn't long before the place was packed.

One day at the coffee shop, we had just finished our latest pieces when we were approached by an older woman who gave us her business card. She had a gallery, she said. She'd been watching us for some time, and liked our work. We had noticed her from time to time, out on the periphery of our vision, sitting quiet and intent. Would we like to do a show featuring our writings and art?

We would. We were delighted, and thanked her profusely.

"What would you like to call it?" she asked.

"The first thing we ever saw together," Stell said thoughtfully.

"Yes," I said. "The moon and the daystar."

Perfect Coffee Lattes

Aurie and Stell love their lattes. Being college kids as well as throwbacks to the Beat Generation, they like it strong. Nothing like espresso to set the tone.

The trick to a good latte is cream, half & half, or milk in your cup first, then slowly pour the coffee on top. This method allows the cream to cook lightly without boiling, and helps it to blend softly with your coffee of choice. Using strong coffee makes for a delightful palette of flavors.

To dress it up a bit, add nutmeg, cinnamon, caramel, or even chocolate as per your taste. A little whipped cream on top and you've got a hot and decadent drink.

Prepare two and experience pure coffee bliss with the one whose soul you love the best.

WINE AND ROSES
Rebecca L. Frencl

*I*t had been years since she'd darkened the door of Nonna's Rose Ristorante. Two years, three months and a few days, to be precise. She'd slammed out of there, calling over her shoulder that he could just drop dead if this place meant more to him than she did. She had dreams and she wasn't going to let him stand in her way. Temper had cauterized the heartbreak. Ambition had taken her from tiny little Bay Springs to Chicago where she'd made a name for herself, her own name, Mia Gerret, not his, as a food critic and cookbook writer. She'd traveled the world—from New York to China, Brazil to Barcelona.

Now, she was back. Nanna Rose, Nico's grandmother, had been closer to her than her own grandparents. It had been she who'd seen her peeking through the kitchen doors when she was barely tall enough to see over the counter. Nanna Rose had shown her how to hold a knife, how to season a dish, and how food was more than just sustenance, but history and family.

Mia could see through the window patrons happily diving into mountains of pasta, chasing meatballs across plates, and sipping glasses of deep red wine. Squaring her shoulders, calling herself six kinds of a coward, she shoved through the door wincing when the bells above jangled.

Josie, at the hostess stand, froze, her automatic smile dropping off her face in shock, her eyes red-rimmed from weeping widened. She dropped her pen and sprang around the little podium, sweeping Mia into a hug that squeezed the breath from her. "Mia," Josie sobbed, "I didn't know if you'd come back, especially after this."

Patrons had stopped slurping up pasta, heads turning in their direction. A squeal, a crash, and Pilar leaped over the shards of her tray. Mia saw to her automatic relief that they were empties before Pilar too piled onto the

Mia hug. The breath she'd regained whooshed out of her again. "Mia!" Pilar kissed her cheeks. "You're home."

"Pilar!"

Mia froze. His voice. Closing her eyes for a moment, she shot a half-smile to Pilar. Better to get it over with now, with witnesses. Pilar peeled herself away. "Hi, Nico." Mia patted Josie on the back, nudging her back to the hostess stand. Cutlery began to clink again, the murmur of conversation and one laugh danced over the room as the diners returned to their meals. She knew a lot of the regulars, knew that there were many whose conversation had now to turned to her. People she knew filled in those she didn't on who she was and why her being there was such a shock. She stood, as if frozen, in place. It was Josie's turn to give her a little push toward the door to the kitchen. She smiled at Mrs. Cassier who reached out to pat her hand as she passed by. Mr. Cassier clucked his tongue and shot her a little frown. Well, she knew not everyone would be happy to see her. Speaking of which...

She nodded to the kid behind the bar. Someone new, but her reputation obviously preceded her. Nico stood, a dishtowel twisted in his hands, in the open kitchen doorway. Red sauce smeared his apron and the bandana tied around his head made him look more like a pirate than a cook. Damn, he looked good.

"You came," he whispered reaching out one hand to take hers. She paused, calling herself a chicken, and took his hand. She could see in his face that he'd seen her hesitation and it amused him. She squelched the desire to snatch back her hand. "I didn't think I'd see you." His voice, deep with just the tiniest hint of Naples in the rising vowels, stroked like silk across her skin.

Deciding that survival was worth more than pride, she tugged her hand back, wrapping it around her purse strap. She shrugged. "Well, Nanna Rose issued a command." She smiled, remembering his grandmother, remembering why she was really there. Grief spiked. "She told me to come and here I am."

Sorrow moved in his dark eyes, made her want to reach out, to soothe. "She would have been pleased." He pushed open the door to the kitchen gesturing her through. Head high, she sailed past him, ignoring the warmth pouring from him when she brushed against him.

The kitchen was so much quieter than she remembered. Some new faces, some old. Gino still stood behind the prep table putting the finishing touches on the dishes lined up for delivery. His eyes were red rimmed and he sniffled every now and again. Nanna Rose had taught him this job, her gnarled hands placing every leaf of parsley, sprinkling every teaspoon of cheese while she spoke of texture, color, and presentation. Every dish wasn't just food, she'd explained, it was family, tradition, love. She sniffled a little herself at the memory.

Mia gave Gino a little wave. His competent hands faltered for just a moment when he saw her. His twin sister, Gina, as tiny as he was huge, nearly dropped her frosting knife. "Well, well," she drawled, swirling frosting onto the cake in front of her. "Look what the will dragged in."

"Gina." Gino's voice was a gravelly warning.

Gina snarled at her brother. She gestured with the knife. "I'm just saying what everyone else is thinking." Her hot dark eyes pinned Mia into place. Nico was a silent presence at her side. "You didn't even come to the funeral." A sob broke her voice.

Mia cleared her throat. "I didn't think you'd all want me there."

Gina whirled, whipping her knife into the wash sink. "Nanna Rose would have wanted you there." She stripped off her apron, throwing it at the dishwasher. The girl snagged it out of the air in a practiced move. "I need some air. I'm taking a break." Gina stormed out the back door, letting in a gust of cool air before the door slammed behind her.

Mia took a deep breath, her hands locked on her purse strap. The scent of garlic, tomato, and olive oil filled her senses. Nico's hands dropped warm and strong on her shoulders. "She's taking it hard," he murmured, steering her toward the tiny office in the back of the kitchen. "We all are."

Mia nodded around the hard lump that had formed in her throat. It was too much. She never should have come back. Too many memories crowded her here. Too many dreams had shattered like Pilar's glassware at her feet. The scents, the sights, and the feel of his hands on her—it was just too much. He closed the door behind them, trapping her.

"I need…" she gasped, tears blurring her vision, "I need…"

"To sit down before you fall down," he snapped.

Temper burned through the tears. "You can't tell me what to do," she flared.

He laughed, leaned against the desk at his back. "I never could," he murmured. Bending, he plucked a water bottle from the small fridge under the desk. "Do you want to know what she left you?"

Mia dropped to the chair, accepted the water bottle and rolled it against her forehead. "No." She closed her eyes. "I really don't care, Nico." She opened her eyes, looked up at him. He'd pulled the bandana off his head and the lamplight painted red highlights in his dark hair. His eyes, always sleepy looking, looked heavier than usual as if the weight of the world had settled in them. "I wouldn't be here now if I hadn't gotten her letter."

He nodded, dropped to a crouch beside her. "She told me—" he swallowed "—right before the end that she'd written to you." He reached out as if he'd touch her, but dropped his hand. "I'd hoped…" He leaned back, jerked a thumb over his shoulder in the direction of the kitchen.

"Why don't we talk later?" He took her hand, yanked her to her feet. "Come back after closing. We'll talk. I'll cook for you."

A flutter, nerves or desire, rippled in her stomach, but she nodded. "I'll be back."

He winked at her, tied the bandana back around his head, and gestured her out the door. "Now, get out of my kitchen," he admonished with a smile. "You're distracting my cooks." She couldn't joke, not right now, but she managed a thin smile as she made her way across the kitchen. Gino nodded to her, giving her a small smile. He always had been a soft touch. Gina, however, didn't look up from filling cannoli, her shoulders tight with temper. Nothing soft about her.

***

Bay Springs hadn't changed all that much, she decided. It was still a tiny town on the water. A brisk spring wind danced little white caps on the lake and brought to mind memories of summers on that lake. Sunburn and skinned knees, the scent of sunscreen, cool watermelon and grill smoke curling to the sky. And Nico. He'd always been there. The boy next door, literally, with his tumbled black hair and sleepy dark eyes. The white slash of his grin and his competent hands. Steeling herself against the memories, she turned away from the water, away from the memories. She'd tucked herself into a suite in the only hotel in town the Bayfront Inn. Yet she couldn't settle down, so she'd decided to leave her car in the inn's tiny lot and wander around town.

Finn's Diner still had the same menu posted in the window. She could see Carly, one of her old high school friends, waiting tables behind the plate glass window. She's scurried by without letting her old friend know she was there. Maybe later, if she decided to stay in Bayside, she'd call Carly. They'd go out, wear heels that were too high and drink a little too much. She smiled, the memories smoothing the rough edges. The jagged shards of pain she'd felt when she'd heard of Nanna Rose's death began to settle into place.

She continued to walk. Past the drug store. She wondered if Mack Selkin was still the pharmacist or if he'd given it up and gone to work at the county hospital like he'd wanted to. How many people, she wondered, had had to leave this town to chase their dreams? She paused in front of the library, a tall stone edifice with gargoyles guarding the entrance. When she'd left, she'd have done anything to get away. She'd felt like a wolf in a trap and she'd been willing to gnaw off her own paw in order to get away. She recalled the shattered look in Nico's eyes when he'd first seen her and she wondered for a moment, if she had lost a part of herself when she'd left.

Miss June, the ancient white-haired librarian, recognized her the instant she stepped in and come around the desk to enfold her in a lavender scented hug. "Oh, my Mia," she piped, cradling Mia's face in her parchment dry hands, a smile breaking through the lines crisscrossing her face. "I am so happy to see you, but so sorry for your loss." She tugged Mia around the desk, settled her in a creaking chair and offered her a cup of flowery tea. "I looked for you at the funeral, but I suspect the news came too late for that?" Mia sipped, allowed the tiny fiction between them. Miss June brightened. "I have both your books here." She smiled. "They're very popular with the young brides who want to learn to make something a little fancier than their mama's meatloaf."

"Never thought that a couple of cookbooks could put you on the map." Mia smiled. "I was working on another when I got the call about Nanna Rose."

Miss June sipped. "Italian food this time?" she asked with a small smile.

Mia shook her head. "No, I could never do better than Nanna Rose and those recipes belong to her." And

Nico, she silently added. She'd given up the right to those recipes when she'd left Bayside and him. "No." She returned to the question. "It was a Thai fusion book. Last year, I went on this amazing trip through Southeast Asia and it gave me so many different ideas." Excitement began to bubble. It was so easy to talk food. So easy to wax poetic on flavors, textures, and scent, and Miss June was a perfect audience.

The tea grew cold in her cup as she described the Tedsaban Market in Sakon Nakhon, Thailand. For an hour, she forgot her grief over Nanna Rose's death, her nerves and regrets when she saw Nico, and the eeriness of walking through the town in which she grew up, but no longer belonged.

She bade Miss June a fond farewell, kissing her wrinkled cheek and promising to send her a copy of her new book as soon as she got her first author copies. She strolled through Bay Springs now with a lighter step. Connecting with Miss June felt like it had rooted her a little more firmly.

As the sun set over the water, she allowed the nostalgia to wash over her. Nico was everywhere. She paused at the gazebo in the park where he'd first kissed her, admired the new scoreboard over the football field at the high school they'd both attended, and walked out to the end of the pier where he'd caught her and Carly skinny dipping after midnight and had joined them after a cheeky dare. She wouldn't fight with him, she resolved. No matter how he provoked her, and Lord knew he could raise her blood pressure with a look, she wouldn't argue. She wouldn't let him bait her. She'd go to dinner and hear what he and his grandmother had to say before she returned to Chicago to her books and her passport. She ignored the little pang in her heart at the thought of leaving again and never returning.

***

The shades had been pulled on Nonna's Rose Ristorante, yet golden candlelight seeped around the edges. The doorbell jangled when Mia entered. Most of the lights were out; only the back wall sconces and the candles on one table were lit. Everything else was tucked away for the night. Quiet music drifted from the propped open kitchen door. Sinatra's voice, rich and soaring, drew her back to where the lights shone brightly and the scents of sauce and garlic lingered in the air.

Nico stood dressed in dark jeans and a blue shirt open at the throat and rolled up at the elbows. He'd tied his hair back and he hummed along with Sinatra. She saw when he sensed her presence. The swift rocking of the knife through parsley stopped for a second, then resumed. He nodded to the wine glass at his elbow. "I poured you a glass. I remembered you didn't like Chianti, so it's a nice cabernet."

She drifted closer, picked up the glass. "Thank you." She sipped, enjoying the velvet slide of the wine, oak and fruit lingering on her tongue. "Need a hand?"

He jerked to the sauce simmering on the stove. "Take a look at that, would you?"

She nodded, wandered over her glass in one hand, a wooden spoon in another. "Nanna's sauce?" She smiled as the aroma washed over her.

"It seemed appropriate."

She stirred, sipped. "Did she…" She clamped her lips shut, moved to the station next to him and began to shred the Romano waiting there.

He turned, leaning hip shot against the counter, the glass looking very fragile in his grip. "Did she ask for you at the end?" He sipped, pinning her with those dark eyes. "She did, but she knew that she wouldn't be able to make it that long." He set the wine to the side. "She said she'd waited too long." He grinned, running a hand through his hair, pulling out the band holding it back. "She then slapped me on the back of the head and told me to not make the same mistake."

Her hands froze on the cheese and grater. "What…"

"She left you half the restaurant." If he'd hit her over the head with the serving platter he pulled down from the shelf, she'd have been less shocked. "She gave to it you and me."

Steam billowed as he poured handmade linguine on the platter. She moved on automatic, years of working at his side as a line cook for his grandmother had her pouring fragrant sauce over the pasta, her body moving even as her mind clicked off. "Me?" She put down the pot before she dropped it. "Nico, I…" The words dried in her throat as he reached around her to pick up a handful of cheese. His chest pressed against her back as he sprinkled Romano over the dish.

"Grab the bread." He lifted the platter over her head turning away, making her feel suddenly cold.

She grabbed the bread and wine glass, following him into the dining room. She took a bracing sip. "Do you want me to sign over my half the restaurant?"

He settled in a chair dishing up pasta, a dull gold ring glinted in the flickering candle light. "I have some papers here for us."

She accepted the plate, settled across from him. "Did she suffer?" she asked, twirling pasta on her fork.

He caught her gaze from over the rim of his wine glass. "No." He set the glass aside, topped them off. "She just drifted off the day after she slapped me. It was very peaceful." He scooped pasta onto his own plate. Broke off the heel of the bread and handed it to her. "It would stand to reason that her last act on earth was to smack me." He rubbed the back of his head. "My mother laughed and said it was so appropriate for her mother." He dipped bread into sauce. "She found her the next morning. Went in to give her coffee and she was gone."

Mia smiled. "I thought she might have waited until after her coffee." Nanna Rose had been a caffeine addict. They'd shared many a cup over a gossip. The percolator had always been bubbling away on the back of the stove.

He gave a choked laugh, sobered. "She kept all your postcards. No matter where you sent them from, all those exotic places. She kept them. She missed you."

Mia looked down at her plate, put down her fork. "I missed her too."

His hand covered hers, warm and solid. "I missed you too."

She gasped, her eyes whipping up to his. "Nico, we…"

He nodded. "If you want to sign over your half of the restaurant, you can sign the papers." He let her go; reached back pulled a stack from a nearby chair. "But if you want to give up on Nonna's Rose, there are some other papers you need to sign first." He handed her a thin packet with her name on it.

Her heart hammered in her chest as she read. She reached out, drained her wineglass. "I shouldn't be surprised," she managed to squeeze out of her throat. She trailed a finger over the papers, divorce papers. "I kept expecting them from you."

His gaze held hers for a moment. "I kept expecting them from you." He gestured with his fork. "You were the one who left."

She gripped the papers, crumpling them. "I needed to get away. I was drowning here. All you wanted was the Rose and I needed…"

"More than I could give you." His voice, thick and warm, trailed up her spine. He could always make her want him even when she hated him. "Sign those and the restaurant papers and you're quit of me. There wouldn't be anything tying you here."

She remembered the words that she'd thrown at him

when she'd left. The tears, the heartache. He'd been everything she'd wanted at eighteen and nothing she'd needed at twenty-two. She'd seen her dreams of travel disappear in a tide of spaghetti sauce and olive oil. She needed to see, to do, and to write and dream and she was afraid that if she stayed she'd wind up hating him and he'd wind up hating her. So, she'd left. Yet, she'd never really freed him, she realized. Even as she'd removed her ring, tucked it in the very back of the jewelry box, she hadn't wanted to break that last bond.

"I thought..." She stood, needing to move.

He pushed away from the table toward her. He grabbed her arms turning her to look at him, making her look at him. "You thought I'd just send them to you, so you could sign them and not have to come back here. Not have to look at me or your past."

Tears spilled from her eyes. Dean Martin's voice, "That's Amore" soared over them from the restaurant speakers. "I knew if I came back here I'd..." she stuttered to a stop, her eyes widening at what she'd almost admitted. Her heart hammered in her chest as he tightened his grip.

"You'd what?" The papers fell from her fingers as he pulled her closer, crushed under his shoes.

She felt the smile as he reeled her in. "I knew," she whispered against his lips, "that I'd never want to leave again." The words vibrated down to her toes. "I've traveled all over the world, Nico, but there's nowhere else in the world that feels more like home that right here." She took the final step that closed the distance between them. Fitting, since she'd taken the first steps away.

A thousand miles, so many empty years, and a novel's worth of harsh words disappeared in the heat of his kiss, the press of his body against hers. He ripped his mouth away from hers on a groan, dropping his head to bury his face in the juncture of her neck and shoulder, his breath dancing shivers down her spine. "It was everything I could do to not grab hold of you the second I saw you this afternoon and beg you not to go." He hands ran down her back, pressing her against him. "Tell me to rip up the divorce papers, Mia. I won't stand in the way of your dreams, your career. I promise, no matter where you need to travel, I'll be here waiting for you."

She pressed her face to his shirt, holding him as tightly as he held her. She smiled against his chest. "I've seen everything I want to see in the world, Nico." She pulled back, looked up at the boy she'd loved, the youth she'd married and the man she wanted. She'd started to come home a dozen times in the last year. She'd woken in Bangkok in an empty hotel bed and wondered what Nico would think of this place. Nanna Rose's letter. She pulled back. "I need to show you something." She reached into the purse she'd tossed on the bar when she'd walked in, pulled out Nanna Rose's letter. "Here, read this."

He took the letter, read it. His grandmother's lily perfume rose from the pages and brought her back. For a moment, Mia thought she could hear the clink of Nanna Rose's many bracelets, could smell the scent of lilies and coffee that seemed to trail behind her and she knew that Nanna Rose was still with them. Would always be with them.

Nico looked up from the letter. "She knew."

Mia took the letter back, folded it carefully, and put it away. "That I still loved you?" She nodded. "Yes, she knew. She said she could tell in every word I wrote in my books and in my postcards. I love that she told me to stop being a fool and to come home. She had one last gift for me."

He smiled, reached out to take her hand in his, tug her against him. "The restaurant," he nodded.

She shook her head. "No, Nico, not the restaurant. You. You're my gift." She pulled him close. "I'll come home, Nico, no matter where I travel. I want to come home.

To you."

Jerry Vale's "Volare" poured into the dining room as he pulled her close. Candlelight beat against the windows of Nonna's Rose and wine grew warm in glasses. They ripped up both sets of papers, stuffing them gleefully into the paper shredder in the office. They sat over a plate of biscotti and cups of strong coffee making plans, exchanging heated glances, and arguing over the placement of the new wine lockers. Mia could swear that she could smell Nanna Rose's perfume when she got up for a refill on her coffee. She glanced over her shoulder at Nico, bent over the plans they'd scrawled on the back of a placemat. Mia knew that Nanna Rose would approve.

Nonna's Rose Ristorante Marinara Sauce

Ingredients:
1-2 pounds of Roma or plum tomatoes
2-3 tablespoons olive oil
2 teaspoons salt
2 tablespoons fresh minced garlic
2 tablespoons fresh oregano
2 tablespoons fresh basil
1 tablespoon fresh parsley
¼ cup red wine (something you'd drink)

Directions:
1. Preheat the oven to 450 degrees.
2. Quarter the tomatoes, removing the stems and ends. This works best in a glass baking dish.
3. Add the rest of the ingredients and toss until the tomatoes are well covered.
4. Cook down the tomatoes, stirring occasionally for 40-45 minutes, until the tomatoes have pretty much turned into mush and the edges are just starting to blacken.
5. Puree the tomato mixture--you can use a regular blender or an immersion blender until you have a creamy sauce.

The marinara can be frozen for up to six months, or canned and kept for a year (though it's never lasted that long in my house). It's a great way to use all the tomatoes from a summer garden. The sauce has a creamy consistency that brings to mind a vodka sauce without any of the guilt of a cream sauce. It works best over simple pasta with some good sharp Romano cheese.

Grandma's Meatballs

Ingredients:
ground chuck
Romano cheese
minced garlic
chopped parsley
garlic powder
bread crumbs
1 egg per pound of meat

Directions:
As with a real grandma's recipe, it's merely a list of ingredients that you adjust for how many meatballs you'd like to make. One pound of ground chuck makes about 15 meatballs the size of golf balls. Add the cheese and parsley to the meat by the handful. You should be able to smell the garlic, but it shouldn't be overwhelming. Usually it's a couple of teaspoons of the minced garlic. The powdered garlic is to add if you need a little more. It mixes in well without leaving big chunks of garlic. One egg, lightly beaten, per pound of meat. Add bread crumbs until the mixture is moist--not too wet or dry. Form the meatballs into 1 ½ inch balls and bake on a lined cookie sheet for 15 minutes in a 400 degree oven. Add them to the sauce for your favorite pasta or sandwich.

New Future
K.C. Sprayberry

~Keri~

*T*he craziness that was the lives of my family is still long from over, but I'm trying to forget all that tonight. Today is Saturday. The date is February 14, the most romantic day of the year, and I'm more than ready to celebrate with my bestie and our boyfriends. Specifically, my bestie will show up at my house with my guy, to meet her guy and me for a romantic dinner. Oh, did I mention how her guy just happens to be my twin?

"Hey." Shane darts in the back door, a dozen grocery bags dangling from one hand. "Smells fabulous. What is it?"

"A surprise." My hands shake as I slice into the strawberries that I've picked out of the basket I got at the fruit market this morning. "If this part works."

"Hey." He covers both my hands with one of his. "It'll work, little sis. Don't push yourself so hard."

He's still very overprotective of not just me but of Kenny, Jimmy, and Stacy. We still have nightmares from the four-month long captivity we went through when El Creepo took us from our family. It's only been a little under two months since we came home. Mom is the only person who agrees with my idea for tonight. She took the four younger kids to her parents for a night of fun while Shane and I prepare a meal that cements the relationships we feel we can finally move forward with, without the worry that our dad will mess things up.

"I'll be okay." My voice says that but my hands still shake at the worst possible moment. "Maybe."

"Let me do those." He takes the knife from my hand and begins the delicate task of creating fans from the berries. "Dipping these in chocolate?"

"Yeah." I point at a small pot of chocolate on a back burner of our new stovetop. "They'll go on the dessert once they're cool."

This stovetop is a totally amazing piece of work we were able to get thanks to the assistance of a lot of people. It has a grill on one side, six burners, and a matching set of ovens placed into the wall between the kitchen and the pantry. Even though it's February, big bro and I are putting on a meal that is fabulous in the summer.

"Great." He jerks his head at the fridge. "Pull the steaks out so they're ready for the grill. And I got salad stuff. Can you do that and one of your fabulous dressings?"

A glance at the clock reassures me that we have the time. Shane and I spend a lot of time in the kitchen, now that he, Mom, and I aren't in survival mode trying to earn enough money and take care of the little ones. Our family of seven happy people wasn't possible until recently, and we're still getting used to it. Before that happens, though, I want tonight to be perfect, and for Axe to realize I'm not a fragile china doll, ready to shatter into a million pieces if something goes wrong.

~Shane~

I glance at little sis, still not sure if I can let her out of my sight for more than a minute. Her nightmares are legendary; enough that the neighbors have called the cops on a couple of occasions when her screaming sounded like the world was coming to an end. Tonight is her idea, her way of trying to prove to me, my girl, Carly, and Keri's guy, Axe, that she's going to be fine. I know Keri will be fine, one day, but I think she's still trying too hard to shove the emotional pain she went through when El Creepo ripped her and three other siblings away from our home.

"What kind of dressing?" Keri holds scissors over

our herb garden, now taking over the shelves between the stove and dining area. "I was thinking basil and maybe some tarragon."

"Works for me." I finish slicing the strawberries and dip them in warm, melted chocolate, fanning them out and laying them on waxed paper. "We now have salad, and dessert, and the steaks won't take a minute or two on the grill."

"For you and Axe maybe." She throws me a saucy grin. "Carly and I don't want to kill our food before we eat it."

"Okay." I throw up my hands in defeat. "I'll kill your food. And Carly's."

"Good." She snips off basil and tarragon, carefully cleaning the leaves and inspecting each one for any imperfections.

Now, if it had been me, I would have picked up a store brand dressing and that would have been it, but Keri wants everything to be perfect. So far it is… except for the dessert, a cheesecake she's been playing with for a month now, trying out different versions on the family. Reactions have varied from Mom's "fabulous, don't change a thing" to the little ones wrinkling their noses and proclaiming "Yuck!" Our four younger siblings are more ice cream sundae types than cheesecake anyway.

"So, what variation of the cheesecake did you decide on?" I ask.

"You'll see." Keri is being enigmatic, which kind of freaks me out. "It's a surprise."

"Okay." I rummage around in the fridge, searching for a snack to hold me over until the others get here. "What's this?"

I back away, holding a platter of green beans and carrots wrapped in thin slices of ham. A closer examination has me whistling appreciation.

"Prosciutto vegetable wraps?" I ask.

"Before dinner snack," she says. "You need to lightly grill those before you do the steaks. I'll set up the tray."

"And you're going to dress when?" I ask.

"Soon." She glances at the clock. "Okay, soon is here." Keri shoves four salads into the fridge and races toward the stairs. "Don't peek at the cheesecake."

Of course I peek at the cheesecake and have to slap my own hand to keep from trying it.

Smells great. Looks great. Keri has her groove on today.

~Keri~

My hands are shaking again. I was okay in the shower, even great when I dried and styled my blond hair into a curly side ponytail, but now that I'm pulling on the pink puffy sleeved tunic and black leggings I bought to impress Axe, I can't stop shaking.

It's Axe. He's a great boyfriend. We've been on dates. Why am I so scared?

I've never talked about my fears left over from the kidnapping. Everyone thinks I'm back to the normal Keri they've always known. There are a few scars from that time, mostly scratches that got infected, but most of the scarring is inside, to the part of me that used to believe everything would turn out great.

"Tonight will turn out fabulously." I shake a mascara wand at my mirror. "Don't jinx this. Nothing bad will happen."

That helps me get past putting on makeup and sliding large gold hoops into my ears. Balancing on the end of my bed, I slip on the ankle boots Mom bought me last weekend and examine the result in the mirror.

"Totally hot, girl!" I give myself a thumbs up and head for the door, but can't walk through it.

Visions of how slowly Axe moved with our relationship run through my head. He was a total doll from the moment we got together in the crazy days after our rescue in northern Arizona. Axe didn't once push me too much. Our first official date was an afternoon of miniature golf at Sir Gooney's with my four younger brothers and sisters. His totally cool way of including them made me love him more than I already did, and I began trusting a few people outside my family. We've done a bunch of double dates with Shane and Carly, mostly just walking around town or hanging at McD's for hot chocolate and pies.

Tonight is a promise to myself that I will take our relationship to the next level. For most girls, they might be considering sex. I'm just thinking about the first kiss and no further. All I want is for my guy to hold me in his arms and kiss me. But I can't walk out of my bedroom and go downstairs to make sure Shane hasn't messed up the dinner I've been planning for a month

Isn't that the silliest thing?

~Shane~

Deciding that Keri is freaking out, I do a quick grill of the prosciutto snacks and arrange them on a tray that I put on the table, adding some of the heirloom grape tomatoes she didn't need for the salad. The sound of a car stopping outside the back door brings a smile to my face and I slap the steaks onto the grill.

"Smells great." Carly, my girl, bounces over and hugs me from behind. "Is girlfriend still getting ready?"

"Might be." I glance over my shoulder at her smiling face. "Or she might need some advice from her bestie."

"Anything, tall and cute." Carly tries to get away with a peck on my cheek.

I hold out the grill tongs to Axe and feel him take them. Then I give Carly a proper kiss, one that proves to her once and for all that I love her for who she is. I don't care if she's African American and I'm Anglo. Big deal. She's a fabulous friend to little sis and the best girlfriend in the galaxy to me.

"Wow." She steps back and stares at me with wide eyes. "That was some kiss."

"Yup." I grin at her. "Want to tell Keri to hurry?"

"Sure, tall and cute." Carly's exit from the kitchen is slow, her eyes lingering on me for a couple of heartbeats longer than usual.

"Looks like Keri did a great job." Axe flips the steaks. "Everything smells great."

"Yeah." I open the fridge to display the four cheesecakes sitting on the top shelf. "I don't know what she did with these, but they smell great."

"Really?" He walks over to take a sniff. "Oh, wow. I want those now."

"So do I." I shut the door. "But we gotta wait."

"Yeah, that's getting hard. I got Keri something special." Axe gives me the tongs to show me a box.

It's not much of a box, actually it's kind of plain looking, but when I see what he's got inside, I can't help but whistle.

"She'll love it." I say a prayer of thanks that Axe didn't go with a dumb, girly gift. "Where did you find it?"

"At What's Old Is New Again." He sets the box beside one of the plates. "Is she okay today?"

"Just like most days," I admit. "Doing too much. Trying to cover how scared she still gets."

"I think that'll change tonight." He puts a flash drive in the stereo and cues up some soft music. "Starting with this."

"Cool."

The two of us make sure the food is on the table and

listen for the sound of footsteps on the stairs.

~Keri~

I'm still standing in the doorway when my bestie comes up the stairs. Carly takes one of my arms and gently tugs.

"You're not bailing tonight, girlfriend." She looks my outfit up and down. "Totally hot. Axe will love you more than he does now."

My smile shakes a little, but I'm feeling more secure. Carly takes hold of one of my hands and gently tugs.

"Don't let that man win, girlfriend," she whispers. "I get that you're still scared. You can't hide that from me, but we're here for you. All of us care. We want you to be the same fearless Keri that he took away from us."

Step by step, we move into the hallway. I draw in a breath and let it out when we start down the stairs. It's hard to think, hard to do anything but remember the nightmares I don't tell anyone about, even Shane, although I'm sure he shares them with me. To give myself time to find my center again, I concentrate on her outfit.

She's totally hot in a short skirt in a mad pattern of blues and reds, with a white bustier style top and a jeans jacket with rolled up sleeves. Carly took my advice and went with open toed ankle high boots to complete her outfit. With her dark brown skin and shoulder length straight black hair, she's probably the most beautiful senior at Landry High.

"Nearly there." Her voice penetrates the hazy fog of better times.

"Axe will think I'm mental," I whisper.

"No he won't," she says. "He thinks you're the prettiest, strongest girl in the world."

"Really?"

"Really."

I forget all about being scared of a past that still haunts me. My focus is on the guy standing at the bottom of the stairs, his eyes lighting up when he sees me, and my world narrows to this one guy.

"Hey," he says.

Carly squeezes around Axe and darts off in the direction of the kitchen. I go down the last couple of steps and he puts an arm around my shoulder.

The warmth, a feeling of security, all of that and more gives me back my confidence.

"You look so good." He walks with me toward the kitchen. "Shane told me you made those prosciutto wraps. Really good."

Okay, I can talk about food. I love cooking. I love creating new things out of old recipes. Food is safe.

"Thanks." I smile up at him. "You look good."

We keep up the small talk, the frozen feeling inside me vanishing a little more with each silly comment.

The smell of perfectly seasoned steaks breaks the mood.

"You better kill those steaks, tall and cute," Carly says. "You know Keri and I don't like our meat to moo back at us."

I can't help it. She says that exact same thing when we barbecue in the backyard during the summer. My laughter breaks the quiet and then Axe is laughing and the awkward moment is long gone.

~Shane~

Man, I can't believe how everything went from tense to laughing in just a second, and all thanks to my girl. All of us are talking and acting like last summer never happened. Keri keeps touching Axe, smiling up at him, acting like she's been his girlfriend forever. Even our twin bond isn't full of uncertainty and fear.

Little sis is going to make it. She's going to survive.

"Hey, beautiful." I tug on my girl's hand. "Let's get the dessert while those two talk."

"They're not talking." Carly's whisper doesn't quite work.

"We're talking." Axe doesn't look away from Keri. "Just not a language you understand."

"Oh. Em. Gee." She rolls her eyes and goes into the kitchen with me.

We get the cheesecakes out of the fridge and put them on plates. Carly carefully lifts a strawberry to lay it in the center and I add some chocolate curls.

"That smells better than good," she says. "What did Keri use in this recipe?"

"No clue," I admit. "She chased me out of the kitchen while she made this. Smells astral."

I'm pretty sure it'll taste better than it smells. Cheesecake is little sis' best dessert. She can take the most basic recipe and somehow she makes it utterly fabulous with just a few twists, like using powdered sugar instead of granulated, or changing flavorings. This Marble Cheesecake is a family favorite, but it has never smelled this good before.

Carly and I make it back to the table right as Keri opens the gift that Axe brought for her. I set down the food I carry and hold my breath. My best bud and I weren't sure but this has to be the one gift little sis will love. It's not ordinary but it's also not too weird.

"Ohhh!: Keri holds up the necklace and breaths out. "Oh, it's… it's…" She smiles at Axe. "It's gorgeous. Can you please put it on?"

He does as Carly and I sit down. I watch the moment, understanding that I might not be able to sense how little sis feels but that I approve. The necklace that ends right below her collarbone is a mix of a thick, old gold tone chain and a black ribbon with gold links on it. There are hearts, and small pearls, and tiny pink bows hanging all around one large heart that says "Be Mine."

Carly touches my hand and I glance at her, reaching into a pocket to pull out a small promise ring that I bought her last week. I slip it onto her ring finger.

"Tall and cute, Oh. Em. Gee!" Her smile is huge. "Are you serious?"

"It's a promise to be in a committed relationship," I say.

"Yes. I know." She glances from the ring to me. "Yes."

I get what she's saying. Our relationship didn't start out at the best possible moment, but we've changed so much since that awful hot August night. I can't imagine any other girl in my life, but I have the rest of high school to get through and then college.

~Keri~

Shane and Carly chased Axe and me out of the kitchen. We're in the living room, swaying slowly to some old love song. His hand against the small of my back is so warm, feels so right.

Axe stares into my eyes, capturing the part of my heart I thought had frozen forever. His head lowers as the music switches to "Kiss From a Rose" and his lips capture mine.

Both of his arms are around my waist now, lifting me as we kiss. We're turning in a slow circle and I release the last of the sadness ruling my head and heart. I know now that this is what I've always wanted, the love of a guy willing to stay with me through the dark nights.

~Shane~

My twin bond explodes and I have to look at what's happening. There is unbridled joy, happiness that I've never felt from Keri before. I turn to go back into the living room, but Carly is there, pulling me into a corner and demanding that I pay attention to her.

"Love you, tall and cute," is all she has to say.

I kiss my girl, not for the first time, but with an intensity letting her know that I will always love her.

Marble Cheesecake

Crust:

1 ½ cups graham cracker crumbs
6 tablespoons melted butter
¼ cup granulated sugar

Combine ingredients well. Press into bottom and up sides of greased 9" cheesecake pan, or into miniature cheesecake pans. Chill crust for 5-10 minutes in freezer or bake for 10 minutes in a 350 oven.

Cheesecake:

3 squares (3 ounces) unsweetened chocolate
1 teaspoon vegetable shortening
2 pounds cream cheese
2 teaspoons vanilla extract (or your favorite flavoring)
1 ½ cups granulated sugar
6 large eggs, slightly beaten
2 cups light cream or 1 cup heavy cream and 1 cup milk

Preheat oven to 450 degrees.

Melt the chocolate with shortening in the top of a double boiler.

In a large mixing bowl, beat the cream cheese and vanilla (or other flavoring) until light and fluffy.

Slowly add the sugar and then the eggs. Beat just until well blended. Stir in cream.

Place about 3 cups of the cream cheese mixture in a separate bowl and add the melted chocolate. Blend.

Pour the plain cream cheese mixture into the prepared crust. Add the chocolate mixture by dabbing spoonfuls on top in about 3 different spots. Use a knife or spatula to swirl the chocolate mixture through the white mixture in a zigzag pattern, marbling the cake, but don't disturb the crust. (If making individual cheesecakes, divide plain cheesecake mixture into four small pans, and then add smaller spoonfuls of chocolate mixture to those before marbling.)

Bake for 15 minutes at 450 degrees then reduce temperature to 300 and bake for about an hour. Smaller cheesecakes will take less time, so watch during this time. Allow the cake to cool in the oven for 30 minutes and then cool to room temperature. Chill.

Meet the Authors:

Mya O'Malley:

Mya O'Malley was born and raised in the suburbs of New York City, where she currently lives with her husband, daughter and three step-daughters. The family also consists of two boxers, Destiny and Dolce and a ragdoll cat named Colby. Mya earned an undergraduate degree in special education and a graduate degree in reading and literacy. She works as a special education teacher and enjoys making a difference in the lives of her students.

Mya's passion is writing; she has been creating stories and poetry since she was a child. Mya spends her free time reading just about anything she can get her hands on. She is a romantic at heart and loves to create stories with unforgettable characters. Mya likes to travel; she has visited several Caribbean Islands, Mexico and Costa Rica. Mya is currently working on her fifth novel.

Facebook fan page: www.facebook.com/myaomalley
Twitter: https://twitter.com/MyaOMalley

Rocky Rochford:

My name is Rocky Rochford and I am a Scuba Diving, Photo taking, Adventure Seeking, Sword Collecting, Writer & Marine Conservationist. I'm a handful of years into my twenties, but after living life on the road, going town to town before finally settling down, I've gained great insight into the world and her workings. From Day 1 I have been a Writer and a Writer I shall forever remain.

I like to consider myself to be a Student of Everything, and yet a Master of Nothing, who does not choose what he writes, but writes what chooses him, be it fantasy, crime, poetry, philosophy or even adventure. After all life is a journey we all get to experience, just like a good book.

Every read of one of my typed works, is another trip into the imagination of my mixed up, crazed and deranged mind. Welcome to the World of Rochford.

Facebook:
https://www.facebook.com/IamRockyRochford?fref=ts

Twitter:
https://twitter.com/search?q=%40RockyRochford&src=typd

Susanne Matthews:

Susanne Matthews was born and raised in Cornwall, Ontario, Canada. She loves history and suspense, especially when she can combine the elements. She's an avid reader of all types of books, but has a preference for happily ever after romances. In her imagination, she travels to foreign lands, past and present, or soars into the future. A retired educator, she focuses on her writing, so she can share new adventures and heroes and heroines with her readers. She loves the ins and outs of romance, and the complex journey it takes to get from the first word to the last period of a novel. As she writes, her characters take on a life of their own, and she shares their fears and agonies on the road to self-discovery and love, solving simple and complex problems along the way. When she isn't writing, she reads, enjoys her grandchildren, and values her quiet time with her husband.

Facebook: https://www.facebook.com/SLMauthor
Twitter: https://twitter.com/jandsmatt

Rachael Stapleton:

Rachel Stapleton spent her youth cultivating a vivid imagination inside the book lined walls of an old Victorian library where she consumed everything from mystery to biography, creating magical worlds, hidden elevators, and secret spiral staircases. At sixteen, she penned a column for the local newspaper and in 2006, wrote her first book featuring an adventurous librarian. She lives in a Second Empire Victorian with her husband and two children in Ontario and enjoys writing in the comforts of aged wood and arched dormers. She is the author of The Temple of Indra's Jewel and is currently working on a third book in the Temple of Indra series. Visit her website and follow her on social media or sign up at www.rachaelstapleton.com to receive email updates.

Facebook:
https://www.facebook.com/pages/Author-Rachael-Stapleton/137831156290570?ref=hl

Twitter: https://twitter.com/RaquelleJaxson

Elle Marlow:

Elle Marlow lives in Southern Arizona with her husband, kids, four horses and is a grandmother to two beautiful kids. Always inspired by her home state of Arizona, most of Elle's stories are about the west old and new.

Facebook:
https://www.facebook.com/elle.marlow.5?fref=ts

Twitter: https://twitter.com/ElleMarlowWrite

Vanayssa Somers:

Born in a Yukon winter, I moved to beautiful British Columbia as a toddler and grew up in the deep forests of Vancouver Island. Over the years I trained as a Registered Nurse, earned a B.A. in Sociology from University of Victoria, worked as a Reiki Master, Psychic and NLP counsellor. I was blessed to mother a beautiful daughter who, unfortunately, passed away in her twenties. Through that loss I discovered a gold mine of new depth in myself and in life itself, as she returned to visit me and open a new awareness of life after death. The greatest gift of all is life itself. A graduate of The Monroe Institute and a follower of Bruce Moen's books and website, I work in soul retrieval and connection with my family in the Afterlife. I believe romantic love to be one of life's highest experiences. Writing romance is my joy.

Facebook: https://www.facebook.com/vanayssa?fref=ts

Twitter: https://twitter.com/somerstory

Margaret Egrot

I have lived in The United Kingdom all my life. I have worked with the Probation Service, the Police Authority, as a Charity boss, and as a freelance child protection consultant. I currently sit on the boards of two charities: one that runs assessment centres for families experiencing problems, and one that provides services for the elderly (well, you've got to think ahead...)

I enjoy reading and the theatre. I try to keep fit by swimming and racing my cairn terrier round the park. He usually wins.

Facebook: https://www.facebook.com/pages/Margaret-Egrot/1374506486178952

Twitter: https://twitter.com/meegrot

Cynthia Ley:

Cynthia Ley is rooted to the lush forests of the lower Pacific Northwest.
Where there are volcanoes.
And the sea.

Facebook: https://www.facebook.com/groups/cleyfiction4/
Twitter: https://twitter.com/CynthiaLey2

Rebecca Frencl:

I write, I teach, I'm a union rabble rouser... I get work with kids on a daily basis which makes me feel simultaneously very young and extremely old. I grew up on choose your own adventure books, the Dungeons and Dragons cartoon, and polyhedral dice. So, I write fantasy and paranormal romance. It's an eclectic mix, but that's what I love to read. I'm a very firm believer that there is no such thing as someone who doesn't like to read. They just haven't found the right book yet!

2012 *Ribbons of Moonlight*—Best Romance Novel, Solstice Publishing Contest

2014 Author of the Year—Solstice Publishing

Facebook:
https://m.facebook.com/profile.php?id=115163871892050
&__user=1475707543

Twitter: https://twitter.com/rlfrencl

K.C. Sprayberry:

Born and raised in Southern California's Los Angeles basin, K.C. Sprayberry spent years traveling the United States and Europe while in the Air Force before settling in Northwest Georgia. A new empty nester with her husband of more than twenty years, she spends her days figuring out new ways to torment her characters and coming up with innovative tales from the South and beyond.

She's a multi-genre author who comes up with ideas from the strangest sources. Some of her short stories have appeared in anthologies, others in magazines. Three of her books (Softly Say Goodbye, Who Am I?, and Mama's Advice) are Amazon best sellers. Her other books are: Take Chances, Where U @, The Wrong One, Pony Dreams, Evil Eyes, Inits, Canoples Investigations Tackles Space Pirates, The Call Chronicles 1: The Griswold Gang, The Curse of Grungy Gulley, Paradox Lost: Their Path, Canoples Investigations Versus Spacers Rule and Starlight. Additionally, she has shorts available on Amazon: Grace, Secret From the Flames, Family Curse … Times Two, Right Wrong Nothing In Between, and The Ghost Catcher.

2013 *The Wrong One* #7 Preditors and Editors Readers Poll.

2014 *Paradox Lost: Their Path* #3 Preditors and Editors Readers Poll.

Facebook: http://www.facebook.com/pages/KC-Sprayberry/331150236901202

Twitter: https://twitter.com/kcsowriter

.

www.ingramcontent.com/pod-product-compliance
Lightning Source LLC
LaVergne TN
LVHW051127080426
835510LV00018B/2279